SACRED COMMUNITY

SACRED COMMUNITY

by
Jamie Roach

ANCIENT FAITH SERIES

ISBN 978-0-8341-5038-6

Editor: Mike L. Wonch
Cover Design: Arthur Cherry
Interior Design: Sharon Page

Library of Congress Cataloging-in-Publication Data: 2010920643

CONTENTS

6

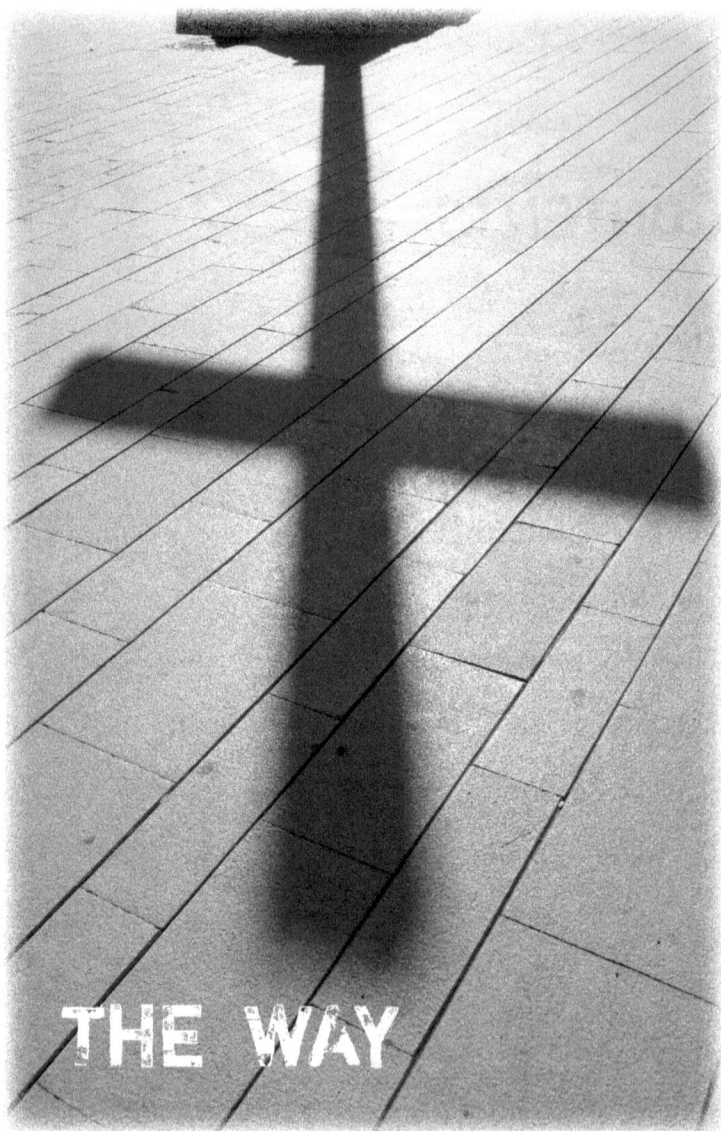

The Way

Do you know what the primary term for identifying the followers of Jesus who made up the early church was? They were simply called "*The Way.*" The Book of Acts uses this phrase 6 times (Acts 9:2; 19:9, 23; 22:4; 24:14, 22). The Way is used 6 times where the term "Christian" is used only once (Acts 11:26).

What can we learn from this title? We must not try to separate faith and works, truth from way, and end from means. Today we have a separation between what a person says they believe and the way they live their lives. For example, do you know people who say they believe in Jesus, but do not follow His teachings and/or example? For most of us it has become acceptable and normal to speak of having "faith in God" without doing the "works of God." You will not find this separation between faith and works in the Bible. Rather than separation, there is integration.

> James says it like this. "*But someone will say, 'You have faith; I have deeds.' Show me your faith without deeds, and I will show you my faith by what I do . . . As the body without the spirit is dead, so faith without deeds is dead.*" —James 2:18-19, 26

Faith is an unseen reality that produces visible works in the world. Just like the body (the part you can see) is dead without a spirit (the part you can not see). In other words, if a person's "faith" in Jesus is not producing the "work" of Jesus, that person has no reason to think their faith can save them. It is a dead, powerless, non-faith.

Paul wrote in Galatians 5:6, "*The only thing that counts is faith expressing itself through love.*" Love is connected to faith. Faith produces love. Acts of love are what people see, but it is produced by faith, which can not be seen. In other words, the Christlike love you express to others is directly connected to your faith in Jesus.

> Jesus said it like this, " *Watch out for false prophets. They come to you in sheep's clothing, but inwardly they are ferocious*

> *wolves. By their fruit you will recognize them. Do people pick grapes from thorn bushes, or figs from thistles? Likewise every good tree bears good fruit, but a bad tree bears bad fruit. A good tree cannot bear bad fruit, and a bad tree cannot bear good fruit. Every tree that does not bear good fruit is cut down and thrown into the fire. Thus, by their fruit you will recognize them."* —Matthew 7:15-20

The true followers of Jesus will be easily identifiable by the fruit their lives produce. Jesus said as much in John 13:35, "*By this all men will know that you are my disciples, if you love one another.*"

Jesus' disciples got the message. They understood that genuine faith (belief) resulted in works, or acts of love. Therefore in the Book of Acts, and in other historical accounts, the early church is identified by the way they lived and not just by what they believed. These followers of Jesus were recognized as "having been with Jesus." They were acting like Jesus. They were living the way He lived. They were called "The Way."

Jesus himself said, "*I am the way, the truth and the life.*" Eugene Petersen points out that only when we put the way of Jesus with the truth of Jesus, do we get the life of Jesus. This journal is all about helping you and your friends live together in the way of Jesus.

I've identified seven ways the early church lived from the Book of Acts. This journal will help you take a closer look at these seven ways and encourage you to figure out together how to live the way of Jesus right where you are.

The way of prayer

The way of restoration (bringing heaven to earth)

The way of sharing

The way of including

The way of suffering and persecution

The way of going

The way of story

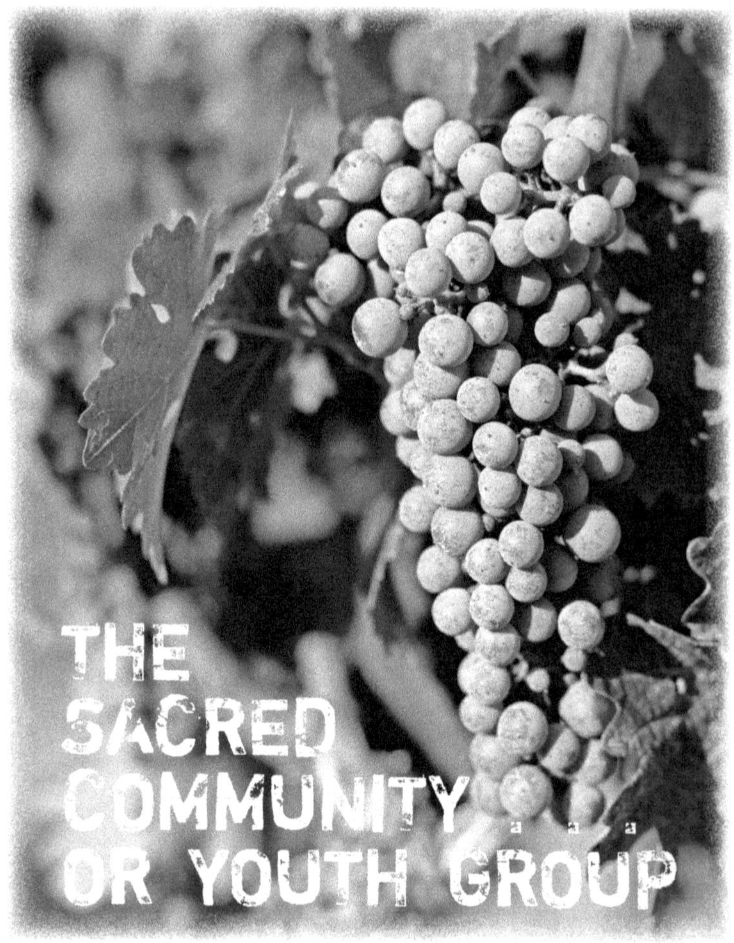
THE
SACRED
COMMUNITY . . .
OR YOUTH GROUP

Each chapter is divided into seven days. Each day is designed to take 10-15 minutes.

Day 1: Preview—This gives you an overview of what you will be looking at for the upcoming week.

Day 2: Meditate—You will meditate on the key scripture(s). Let it seep into your soul.

Day 3: Act—Don't just sit there. Do something. Live it.

Day 4: Reflect—What is your response to the scripture and experience? Pay attention to how you are feeling.

Day 5: Talk—Gather with your friends, grab something to eat, and share together what you are experiencing, learning, and feeling.

Day 6: Transform—Write down your prayers, dreams, thoughts, and feelings as you consider the work of the Holy Spirit in your life.

Day 7: Rest—Sink down into the flame of God's love and allow Him to consume you.

Preview

preview

What is a *sacred community*?

> Sacred: dedicated or set apart for the service or worship of a god.
>
> Community: a unified body of individuals.

A sacred community is a unified body of individuals who are dedicated and set apart for the service and worship of God. There are some big words in that sentence we don't use everyday, so you might want to read it again. If your brain works like mine, read it again slowly. Now ask yourself, does that describe the community at my church?

I want to suggest that there is a big difference between being a "sacred community" and being a "youth group." To be honest, I'm not sure the world needs another youth group. However, I am convinced that a sacred community is exactly what this world needs right now.

I use the term sacred community to refer to the church who is as God intended. I use the term youth group to refer to a sacred community that is either no longer sacred or no longer community, or maybe neither. A youth group is what is left of a sacred community that has lost its vision, mission, and passion.

A sacred community is the Church as birthed by the Holy Spirit in Acts 2. It is a gathering of people dedicated to living the way of Jesus, together. It is a collection of people whose hearts have been knit together, are filled with the Spirit, and embodying the kingdom of God on earth.

Youth Group	***vs.***	***Sacred Community***
Program-centered		People-centered
Exist for self		Exist to make the world beautiful and right again
Lacks real power		Power comes from God's Presence
Inward focused		Outward focused
"Me before we"		"We before me"
Attractional		Missional
Boring		Risky
All about pizza		All about prayer
Fits nicely into pop culture		Challenges pop culture
Marked by cliques and divisions		Marked by unity and togetherness
In-fighting and name-calling		Is a place of peace and grace
Little commitment		Great commitment
Governed by rules		Governed by relationships

meditate

Circle the words or phrases from the list above that best describes your gathering of friends from church. What is missing?

> **Jesus was deeply concerned for the continuation of his redemptive work after the close of his earthly existence, and his chosen method was the formation of a redemptive society. He did not form an army, establish a headquarters or even write a book. All he did was to collect a few unpromising men, inspire them with the sense of his vocation and theirs and build their lives into an intensive fellowship of affection, worship and work.**
>
> **(Elton Trueblood. *Alternative to Futility,* p 29)**

Meditate

The Church as the "New Temple."

> *"Jesus answered them, 'Destroy this temple, and I will raise it again in three days.' They replied, 'It has taken forty-six years to build this temple, and you are going to raise it in three days?' But the temple he had spoken of was his body."* —John 2:19-20

One of the things that got Jesus killed was His teaching that He himself was the fulfillment and replacement for the Holy Temple. What He was saying was, *I am now the place where God's presence dwells on earth. The Temple is about to be destroyed and I am the replacement. If you need healing or forgiveness then come to me. I am filled with God's Spirit (see the story of Jesus baptism) and it is in me that God now dwells on earth.*

That is what John alluded to in John 1:14, "*The Word became flesh and made his dwelling among us. We have seen his glory, the glory of the one and only [Son], who came from the Father, full of grace and truth.*"

No longer were people to go the Temple to offer up sacrifices for sin, Jesus was the ultimate sacrifice for sin. Jesus was now the place where God's glory and truth dwelt on earth. If you needed forgiveness, restoration, and healing, you could find all that and more in Jesus.

Now fast forward to after Jesus' death and resurrection. Jesus is about to go back to sitting at the right hand of God. What does that mean for the presence of God on earth? There is still much pain, suffering, and brokenness. Where does Jesus expect people to go if He is not going to be around?

This scene with Jesus and His disciples reminds me of one of my track meets in high school where I was on the two-mile relay team. Jesus has just finished the third leg of the race and is getting ready to pass the baton on to His disciples. They will continue the race. Listen carefully to His words and see if you don't notice the hand-off taking place.

> *"Again Jesus said, 'Peace be with you! As the Father has sent me, I am sending you.' And with that he breathed on them and said, 'Receive the Holy Spirit. If you forgive the sins of anyone, their sins are forgiven; if you do not forgive them, they are not forgiven.'"*
>
> —John 20:21-23

Pretty amazing stuff don't you think. Jesus was now entrusting the continuation of His ministry to His disciples. For three years they have been following Him, learning to live like Him, to do the things He did. Now He was leaving, but He would still be present by the Holy Spirit living in and through His followers. As they receive God's Spirit, they become the place where God is now dwelling on earth.

To the young community of Jesus' followers living in Ephesus the Apostle Paul wrote,

> *"Consequently, you are no longer foreigners and strangers, but fellow citizens with God's people and also members of his household, built on the foundation of the apostles and prophets, with Christ Jesus himself as the chief cornerstone. In him the whole building is joined together and rises to become a holy temple in the Lord. And in him you too are being built together to become a dwelling in which God lives by his Spirit."*
>
> —Ephesians 2:19-22

Paul was reminding the church in Ephesus that they are now the "holy temple." The word holy means to set apart for a special purpose. It is another word for sacred. In other words, the Church is a holy temple and a sacred community. They are the people of God set apart for a special purpose. Paul further explained that through faith in Christ, and the indwelling of God's Spirit, they have become the place God dwells on earth. In the words God spoke to Abraham in Genesis 12, these people have been "blessed to be a blessing," through them all the world will come to know the healing and saving power of God.

m e d i t a t e

So, what does all this have to do with us and more specifically with your "youth group?" Churches have been passing the baton to future generations ever since. Do you get it? Those who gather together at your church are so much more than just a group of teenagers who get together to eat pizza. God himself has called you out. He has breathed on you His Presence. Together you are the body of Christ on earth, a holy temple, and a sacred community. You have been placed in the midst of darkness that you may shine the light of Christ. All around you are people who are broken, but you have the power to bring healing. You exist in a world filled with unjust systems and practices, but you've been called to live differently and to bring about change so justice can flow like a river.

Read through the Bible verses of this section again. Better yet, use your own Bible and read and underline the verses there. Then answer the following questions.

1. What images do the writers of the Bible use to help explain what the Church is like?

2. How is your view of the Church different today than it was last year?

3. What do you think of Jesus' plan to leave the work of God in the hands of His disciples?

4. Consider how you became a part of God's family. Did it have more to do with a program or building, or did it have more to do with people who loved you and included you on their journey of following Jesus.

THE WAY OF SOFTENING

Do you tend to think about church more as a place, a program or a people?

Is church a place you go or a people you are with?

Do you "go to church" like you go to the movies, or are you part of the church, like you are part of a family?

Act

Huge to being a sacred community is knowing and being known by the other people in the community. I don't mean just knowing names, although for some that may be a great place to start. I'm talking about knowing each other's hopes and fears, successes and failures, strengths and struggles.

When Jesus talks about being friends, He is talking about giving each other the space to be themselves. Too often we put pressure on each other to be someone we're not. What a great gift it is to be truly accepted as who you are. When there is genuine knowing accompanied by grace and acceptance, people are free to take off their masks and be who God created them to be. Our hearts long to be known and accepted as we really are, not just as we hope to one day be.

How well does your sacred community know you?

How well do you know the other people who belong to your sacred community?

Is your community one in which people are truly accepted as they are? Can someone be extremely different from others and at the same time feel like they belong and fit in?

Make a list of all the names of the people in your sacred community. After you have made your list, go back through and pray for each one.

Some things you might consider praying for:

- That they would know and experience God loving them. (1 John 4:16)
- That they would experience God's very best for them in their lives today. (Matthew 6:10)
- That their love for others in the community would increase and overflow. (1 Thessalonians 3:12)
- That their hearts would be filled with compassion for the lost, broken, and hurting people in their midst and around the world. (Matthew 9:36)

Reflect

Go back to page 12 and look over the lists that separate a "youth group" from a "sacred community." After reading through the list again, answer the following two questions.

Is there anything you can do to help your group behave more like a sacred community?

How do you feel about making that change?

Go back to page 13 and re-read each of the scriptures listed that day. When you have finished reading them, answer the following questions.

Which one is your favorite?

Why do you think that is your favorite? What do you like about it?

Think about your experience of praying for your friends and then answer the following questions.

How do you feel about praying for your friends?

What was good about it? What was difficult?

How might your sacred community be different if more people were praying more often for one another?

Being a sacred community is not primarily about a cool youth room, the worship band, the number of kids coming, or your youth leader. It is about everyone organizing their lives around the way of Jesus. It is about living lives of authentic worship, becoming friends who make sacrifices for one another and together being and proclaiming good news wherever you go.

Talk

Becoming a sacred community is not easy. Far too many students settle for just being part of a youth group. One of the things that make true community so difficult is that it requires being vulnerable. To truly know and be known requires that you open yourself up and share how you are feeling and thinking. Opening yourself up like that is a huge risk, one you need to consider carefully before you take it. When you share your thoughts and feelings with others you are giving them something very sacred—a part of who you are. If they don't handle it carefully and with the honor, and with the love and respect it demands, you may get hurt. I'm not trying to talk you out of sharing. Without being vulnerable and honest with one another, true community can never be reached. I just want you to know the risks as well as the rewards.

Discuss as a group:

- Talk together about how your community would be different if it saw itself as a "sacred community" and not just a "youth group."
- What is one thing your group could immediately begin doing that would help define and shape you as a "sacred community?"
- What was your favorite passage of scripture this week and why?
- What was it like for you, praying for others in the community?
- Select one person from the group and have everyone else gather around them. Take time to pray specifically for that person.

THE WAY
OF PRAYER

Transform

So now that you've spent some time thinking about experiencing what it means to be a sacred community, how are you feeling about it? What changes and growth are taking place in your life?

We have begun thinking about a sacred community as being a community of people committed to following Jesus together. Consider your own life and how you are doing at following Jesus. In Matthew 26:58 we read, "*But Peter followed him at a distance.*" If those who know you best were going to describe how you are following Jesus, what words would they use?

How are you doing at following Jesus by surrendering your life to God? Write down one thing you are doing that is helping your relationship with God grow.

How are you doing at following Jesus by loving others in your sacred community?

Write down one thing you are doing that is helping you to love others in your community.

How are you doing at following Jesus by demonstrating compassion to those who are lost, broken and hurting? Write down one way you are becoming a more compassionate person.

Continue to pay attention to what God is doing in your own life. Philippians 1:6 promises that God, who began a good work in you, will continue to work in you until the work is done. Take joy in knowing you are one of God's masterpieces.

> "*Being confident of this, that he who began a good work in you will carry it on to completion until the day of Christ Jesus.*" — Philippians 1:6

Rest

"Be still,

and

know

that

I am

God."

—Psalm 46:10

Preview

"I am the vine; you are the branches.
If you remain in me and I in you,
you will bear much fruit;
apart from me you can do nothing."
—John 15:5

"for I have always been mindful of your unfailing love
and have lived in reliance on your faithfulness."
—Psalm 26:3, TNIV

"but I give myself to prayer"
—Psalm 109:4, ESV

"They all joined together constantly in prayer,
along with the women and Mary the mother of Jesus, and with his brothers."
—Acts 1:14

Of all the Spiritual disciplines, prayer is the most central, because it ushers us into perpetual communion with the Father.
(Richard Foster. *Celebration of Discipline,* p 33)

As we grow in our understanding of prayer, we begin to understand that prayer is not just something we do, it becomes our posture or the dominant attitude of our hearts. Prayer defines our relationship with God. I believe this is what Jesus was getting at in John 15 when He said, *"If you remain in me and I in you, you will bear much fruit; apart from me you can do nothing."* Jesus wants us to understand that He is the source of life. We were created to be in relationship with God. Our position is one of receiving. God pours out himself into our lives and it is up to us to receive Him.

In Acts we learn that the primary thing God wants us to receive is himself, His Presence, and the Holy Spirit. In Him is power and life. Without Him we can accomplish nothing. The Message puts it this way, *"I am the Vine, you are the branches. When you're joined with me and I with you, the relation intimate and organic, the harvest is sure to be abundant. Separated, you can't produce a thing."* (John 15:5-8).

Prayer is an attitude and posture of dependence upon God. So hopefully you can see that our number one priority must be living life intimately connected to Jesus, always receiving from Him his life and power. That is prayer. Prayer is intimacy with God. Although it does include asking God for things we need, it is also so much more than that. Being a father means I buy my kids gifts, but being a father is also much bigger than that.

To the extent that we live our lives in a position of being dependant upon Him, our lives will be fruitful. However, when we get too busy and forget about Him, we begin to live on our own. When we become separated from Him our lives begin to dry up and wither. He is the source of life. In order to experience life, we must remain connected to Him—that is prayer.

Meditate

"*In my former book, Theophilus, I wrote about all that Jesus began to do and to teach until the day he was taken up to heaven, after giving instructions through the Holy Spirit to the apostles he had chosen. After his suffering, he presented himself to them and gave many convincing proofs that he was alive. He appeared to them over a period of forty days and spoke about the kingdom of God. On one occasion, while he was eating with them, he gave them this command: 'Do not leave Jerusalem, but wait for the gift my Father promised, which you have heard me speak about. For John baptized with water, but in a few days you will be baptized with the Holy Spirit.' So when they met together, they asked him, 'Lord, are you at this time going to restore the kingdom to Israel?' He said to them: 'It is not for you to know the times or dates the Father has set by his own authority. But you will receive power when the Holy Spirit comes on you; and you will be my witnesses in Jerusalem, and in all Judea and Samaria, and to the ends of the earth.' After he said this, he was taken up before their very eyes, and a cloud hid him from their sight. They were looking intently up into the sky as he was going, when suddenly two men dressed in white stood beside them. 'Men of Galilee,' they said, 'why do you stand here looking into the sky? This same Jesus, who has been taken from you into heaven, will come back in the same way you have seen him go into heaven.'*

Then the apostles returned to Jerusalem from the hill called the Mount of Olives, a Sabbath day's walk from the city. When they arrived, they went upstairs to the room where they were staying. Those present were Peter, John, James and Andrew; Philip and Thomas, Bartholomew and Matthew; James son of Alphaeus and Simon the Zealot, and Judas son of James. They all joined together constantly in prayer, along with the women and Mary the mother of Jesus, and with his brothers." —Acts 1:1-14

Let's take a closer look at the life of the early church and the way they lived. When Jesus was giving His followers their final instructions on how they were to continue the ministry of redemption and restoration, His number one instruction was "wait for the Holy Spirit to come upon you."

Notice what He did not say. He did not say, "plan a huge event that will attract lots of friends." He did not say, "come up with a really cool name for your group." He did not say, "Go feed the hungry in my name." He did not say, "design a T-shirt for your retreat." No. His initial instructions for His small band of committed followers was go back to Jerusalem and don't move. Stay there and do nothing UNTIL you have received the Holy Spirit.

I remember in high school football going out for a pass, knowing the quarterback was going to throw me the ball. I was wide open with no opposing player between me and a touchdown. I was close enough to our quarterback to see the look in his eyes as he was getting ready to throw the ball to me. We both knew this was going to be a touchdown. And it would have been except for one thing. I got so excited thinking about running down the sidelines racing into the end zone untouched by the other team, that I took my eye off the ball right before it got to me. My eyes glanced downfield toward the goal line and the ball slipped right through my fingers. It was horrible. Everything went into slow motion. One second the ball was in my hands and the next it was slipping through my hands and falling to ground. Without the ball I could do nothing. There was no running, no racing down the sidelines and no touchdown.

A similar thing can happen in the life of our youth group if we are not careful. We get so caught up and excited about what God has called us to do, that we run ahead of Him. Like a receiver racing toward the end zone without the ball, we take off without the one thing we need, the very presence of God.

You can see this in a youth group that is meeting together regularly. They may sing cool songs and have great teaching, but the power and presence of God is not found in their midst. They are running through the motions, but God has been left lying on the field. There is an appearance of ministry happening, but it is hallow and ineffective to bring about any lasting life change.

The power to heal and change lives is in God alone. Jesus knows this. His life was lived in complete and utter dependence upon God. He did nothing He didn't first receive from God (John 5). So we should not be surprised that when Jesus is giving His followers final instructions He said, "Go back to Jerusalem and wait until you have received the Holy Spirit."

Do you see the linkage between prayer and waiting? A big part of prayer is waiting. It is making ourselves available to God. It is a posture and attitude of dependence upon God. I have come to see prayer not as something I do, but as someone I'm with. To pray is to wait with God. It is like the branch "waiting" to receive life and nourishment from the vine. The result is power. Power to live. Power to heal. Power to love. Power to forgive. Power to act and speak in the way of Jesus.

We read in Acts 1:14, *"They all joined together constantly in prayer."* As you read through the Book of Acts you will notice a pattern. It is a cycle of prayer and power. Over and over we see the disciples being in prayer together followed by a manifestation of extraordinary power. It is not us. It is God's Spirit surging through us as we abide in Jesus, that is the source of power. Jesus yielded completely in every way to God's Spirit ("Not my will by thy will be done." Jesus learned obedience through what He suffered). So we too, if we want to realize the fullness of our potential and live into that radical reality God has called us. We must, through prayer, wait upon the Lord until we are clothed with power from on high. If we don't want to be found just running through the motions, we must learn to pray. We must learn to wait together. Anything we can accomplish without God helping us is not worth doing. We have the bold faith to attempt the impossible, with God as our power and strength. Prayer is intimacy with God. When we are intimately joined to God in and through Jesus Christ, His power works in and through us to accomplish His work and purposes in the world. Wait-

ing on God in prayer, often in secret, typically comes right before God's power being seen in public.

Act

This week we are focusing on the "way of prayer." One of the biggest hindrances to prayer is busyness. We simply get so busy that we don't notice what God is doing around us. We are kind of like a cell phone with "no service" or "no signal." We allow the busyness of life to block God's signal from reaching our heart and ears.

Your task for the next 24 hours is to look for those opportunities to pray. Listen for those signals from God. When you normally would have missed them or quickly moved on, this time take a moment to pray and be with Jesus.

For example:

- If you see a breaking news story covering a tragedy taking place, stop and pray for the people involved.
- If you notice a beautiful sunrise or sunset, give God thanks and praise for making it. Let God know how much you enjoyed it.
- When you notice yourself stressing about something, ask God to be with you.
- If you get to do something you really enjoy, like playing a sport or hanging out with friends, realize that too is a gift from God and thank Him for it.
- When a friend shares with you something they are struggling with, pray for them.
- Before you eat a meal, take a second and thank God for providing it for you (keeping in mind there are millions of others who do not have enough food to eat).
- If you do something wrong, admit it and thank God for His grace and forgiveness.

If at anytime you want to talk with God but aren't sure what to say, try praying "*Lord draw near to me as I draw near to you*" (James 4:8a). Many people have found it very helpful to pray simple prayers like that one over and over again as an expression of what they are most desiring in their heart.

Prayer is intimacy with God.

Pray without ceasing.

Call upon God and He will answer you.

I love the Lord because He hears my cry.

Reflect

Before moving on, take some time to carefully consider your thoughts and feelings about prayer. In the same way you may look at yourself in a mirror, take some time look at your heart to see what is there.

> *"They all joined together constantly in prayer, along with the women and Mary the mother of Jesus, and with his brothers."*
>
> —Acts 1:14

Based on what you know of the early church, why do you think they "joined together constantly in prayer?" In other words why do you imagine praying together was so important to them.

Does praying together seem to be as important to churches today? How often do people in your church gather together for the purpose of praying? How important does praying together seem to be to your sacred community? Write down your answers and how you are feeling about them.

Would you like to pray together more or less? If more, what is keeping you from doing it? If less, why?

How did your experiment with listening for God's signals and praying more often go? Did you pray more or less than you did in the previous 24 hours? What did you like about it? What would you do differently next time? Did you sense God was present with you?

What is one way you are thinking differently about prayer these days?

What is one thing you you'd like to change about the way you pray?

Talk

I want you to take time to pray together, using as a guide the prayer Jesus taught His disciples (Luke 11:2-4; Matthew 6:9-13).

The Lord's Prayer: Praying as a sacred community

Before Luke compiled his account we now call the Book of Acts, he wrote down an "orderly account" of the life and ministry of Jesus. In Luke's gospel we read, *"One day Jesus was praying in a certain place. When he finished one of His disciples said to Him 'Lord, teach us to pray.'"*

Can you imagine what that would have been like to sit at the feet of Jesus and learn from Him how to talk with God. The disciples had obviously noticed Jesus praying, and now they wanted to learn how to pray like He did. I think they noticed how Jesus' relationship with God was much more intimate and personal than what they had noticed from the Pharisees. Jesus actually called God, "Abba," which is the equivalent of calling God "Papa" or "Daddy" in our language. No one had ever related to God in such a personal and intimate way before.

I think what the disciples were really asking Jesus was, how can we know God the way you do? How can we talk with Him personally and intimately? I also think Jesus was very excited and glad to teach them. He goes on to teach them what we now call, "The Lord's Prayer." It is called the "Lord's Prayer" because it is how Jesus prayed and how He taught His followers to pray. It is His prayer.

Part 1

Our Father, who art in heaven,
hallowed be thy Name,

The first word of the prayer tells us a lot. It is the word "Our." From the very beginning Jesus' followers understood this prayer was given not given to individuals, but to a community of people who had committed themselves to Jesus and one another. We pray this prayer together as brothers and sisters to our One and Only Father.

When Jesus teaches us to pray "Our Father," He is gently inviting us to see God as our true Father and to understand that we are His children. This phrase teaches us that we belong. We are not strangers, we are family. We have as our Father One who is merciful and gracious. He is filled with compassion, and who is quick to forgive us as well as provide for us everything we need. Therefore let us pray to God with confidence and without fear.

When we say, "hallowed by thy Name" we are recognizing that God is holy. We commit ourselves to keeping God's name holy among ourselves. God is not the best among many gods. He is the One and Only true God. He is unique and set apart. There is no one like Him. His very name should invoke feelings of awe and wonder in our hearts and in our midst.

Scriptures for further reflection
Psalm 103:13
Romans 8:15-16

Part 2

thy kingdom come,
thy will be done,
on earth as it is in heaven.

This is a prayer of surrender. This is a prayer of trust and love. Only the person who truly understands the Father's love and has come to trust Him can pray this prayer of surrender—giving God control of their lives. To invite God's kingdom to come and will be done is to recognize Jesus as the King of your heart and life. As you pray these words imagine yourself stepping off the throne of your heart as you invite Jesus to be the One true Ruler of your life.

Scripture for further reflection

Psalm 103:19

2 Timothy 4:8

Luke 6:46

Part 3

Give us this day our daily bread.

Your Father in heaven wants to provide for you everything you need to live well. Take time to consider what it is exactly that you most need or want. Ask your Father in heaven for what you truly desire. He longs for you to be truly satisfied.

Scriptures for further reflection

Matthew 7:7-11

Psalm 145:15-16

Matthew 6:33

Part 4

And forgive us our trespasses,
as we forgive those who trespass against us.

God has promised that when we confess our sins to Him, He is faithful to forgive us. As we receive God's forgiveness, we are then able to forgive those who have hurt us. As we receive God's love we become the kinds of people who are able to love others from the center of who we are, without faking it. There is no room for judgment, jealousy, anger or bitterness in God's house. As people who have been forgiven much, we must learn to forgive much. Jesus hanging on the Cross offering forgiveness to all who put Him there is our supreme example of what it looks like to forgive.

Scriptures for further reflection

1 John 1:9

Colossians 3:12-14

John 13:34-35

Part 5

And lead us not into temptation,
but deliver us from evil.

Following Jesus is an epic battle. Our world has been hijacked by evil, sin, and death. God has enacted a movement of restoration that will one day be completed. One day, evil will be eliminated and there will be no more death. Until that time He is calling you and me to participate with Him in fighting against evil and to bring about healing and restoration to all that is broken in our world.

We are often tempted to forget our assignment and turn our hearts to lesser things. We often become distracted by things that are not nearly important. We must pray and ask God to keep us from being tempted and distracted by the smaller things of this world.

When we pray, "deliver us from evil," we are asking God to save us from everything that separates us from God and each other. We thank God for the work of redemption He accomplished through His death and resurrection. Also, we ask God to rescue us from the evil that spills out of our own hearts and into the streets of the world in which we live.

Scriptures for further reflection
Ephesians 6:10-13
James 1:2-3

Part 6

For thine is the kingdom,
and the power, and the glory,
for ever and ever. Amen.

We close our time of prayer by recognizing and declaring that Jesus Christ is the King of all Kings and the Lord of all Lords. He has ascended into heaven and sits at the right hand of God. His name is above all names. There is no one like Him.

He alone is God and He alone is the Most High. He is the Lord of all creation and the Savior of the world. Nothing compares to Him. As you pray these closing lines, imagine yourself bowing low before the One true King!

Scriptures for further reflection

Ephesians 3:20-21

Revelation 3:20

Putting it all together.

Take time now to pray this awesome prayer together as a group. Pause between each of the parts giving time for people to share with God what is in their heart, as well as allowing time for God to speak.

Take your time as you pray, linger together in God's presence. Select one person from the group to lead the rest of the group through the prayer, pausing between each part for a time they feel is appropriate.

Our Father, who art in heaven,
hallowed be thy Name,
Pause for people to reflect and think about God as "Holy Father."

thy kingdom come,
thy will be done,
on earth as it is in heaven.
Pause for people to confess "Jesus as Lord" and to surrender their will to His.

Give us this day our daily bread.
Pause for people to ask their heavenly Father for the things they need to live well.

And forgive us our trespasses,
as we forgive those
who trespass against us.
Pause for people to confess sin and receive God's forgiveness and to consider who they may need to forgive or from whom they may need to seek forgiveness.

And lead us not into temptation,
but deliver us from evil.
Pause for people to pray for and seek God's protection and guidance in the choices they make each day.

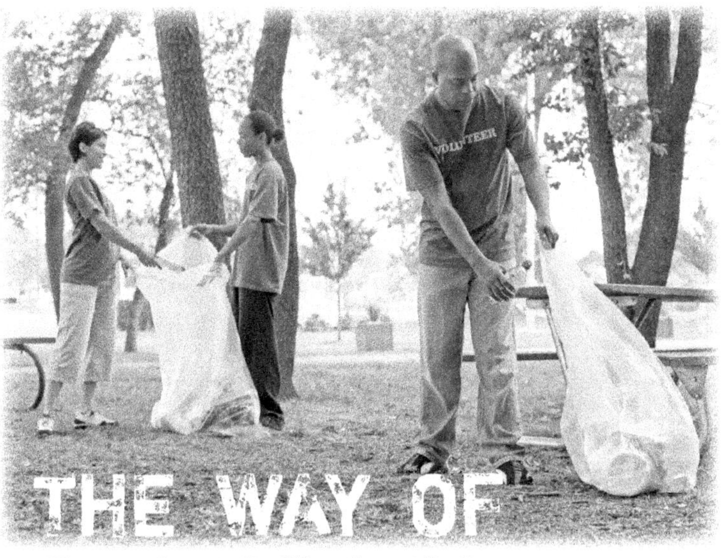

THE WAY OF RESTORATION (BRINGING HEAVEN TO EARTH)

For thine is the kingdom,
and the power, and the glory,
for ever and ever. Amen.
Pause for people to worship Jesus as the King of Kings and Lord of Lords.

Transform

The goal of this journal is not to fill your head with more information, but to be used as a tool in the transformation of who you are.

Our goal is to continually grow and change as we are becoming more and more like Jesus. Take time now to consider where you are seeing growth and change in your own life. Use the categories given to consider how you have changed over the past five years.

	5 years ago	**Now**
Favorite TV Show		
What I did for fun		
My best friend is		
How I was as a friend		
What I thought about God		
How I felt about God		
How I treated my parents		
How I prayed		
How I helped others		

Take time now to write out a prayer that expresses what you are feeling in your heart about how you are growing and developing into the person God created you to be.

Rest

"Be still,
and
know
that
I am
God."
—Psalm 46:10

Preview

Can there be any doubt in our minds that healing was central to Jesus' life and ministry? Over and over in the Gospel the writers record these powerful and life changing words "Jesus healed many." Jesus himself testified, *"On hearing this, Jesus said, 'It is not the healthy who need a doctor, but the sick. But go and learn what this means: I desire mercy, not sacrifice. For I have not come to call the righteous, but sinners'"* (Matthew 9:12-13).

As we discussed earlier, Jesus came into the world to fix it. Through Adam and Eve sin broke and marred God's beautiful creation. God chose and blessed Israel to be a blessing, and through them God would heal and restore all of creation to its former beauty and glory. When Israel failed to be "a light to the Nations" and instead lived as a stiff necked and rebellious people, God threw himself into the mix and became the perfect and faithful Israelite. God himself, in the man Jesus Christ, brings healing and restoration to all of creation. Redemption was enacted on the Cross and through the Resurrection. Paul described Jesus' resurrection as being the "first fruits," meaning more resurrection and new life is to follow. As you are reading this, creation itself is still waiting to be liberated from the bondage of decay (Romans 8:21). Paul wrote that she is crying out in pain waiting for healing and redemption. You and your friends at church are the body of Christ and God longs to bring healing and restoration through the efforts of you and your friends. I wonder if you hear the cries of a broken creation. I wonder if you hear the cries of your fellow classmates who continue to suffer under the pain of loneliness. I wonder if the cries of the sick and hungry have reached your ears, the ones who can bring healing and life.

In Luke 4:18-19 Jesus made His mission and purpose on earth very clear by quoting the prophet Isaiah and claiming these words for himself.

> *"The Spirit of the Lord is on me,*
> *because he has anointed me*
> *to proclaim good news to the poor.*
> *He has sent me to proclaim freedom for the prisoners*
> *and recovery of sight for the blind,*
> *to set the oppressed free, to proclaim the year of the Lord's favor."*

We notice in this text that Jesus was filled with the power of the Spirit. Even Jesus himself did nothing on His own, but only by the power He received as He completely surrendered His will to the Father (John 6:19, 30). He kept His eyes and ears on God and received great power—power to love, power to heal, and power to forgive sins.

Jesus could have used this power selfishly. Immediately before making this declaration, Jesus was tempted for 40 days in the wilderness to do just that. Where else in the Bible do we discover the number 40 and wilderness together? That's right! Israel wondered in the wilderness for 40 years because it failed the test and gave in to temptation. Luke wants us to see that Jesus is the "new Israel" accomplishing what the "old Israel" failed to accomplish.

Jesus' mission was to bring "heaven to earth." Jesus put it this way, "change the way you are living because God's kingdom is now here" (Matthew 3:2; 4:17; Mark 1:15). Every demon cast out by Jesus, every sickness healed, every person loved and included, was a sign and sample of what life is like in God's kingdom.

Meditate

Allow this story from Acts 3 to seep into your soul. Immerse yourself in it and give it time to get inside of you. Before you start reading take one minute to be completely quiet and still before the Lord. Make room for Him in your heart.

> *"One day Peter and John were going up to the temple at the time of prayer—at three in the afternoon. Now a* **man who was lame** *from birth was being carried to the temple* **gate called Beautiful**, *where he was put every day to beg from those going into the temple courts. When he saw Peter and John about to enter, he asked them for money.* **Peter looked straight at him**, *as did John. Then Peter said, 'Look at us!' So the man gave them his attention, expecting to get something from them.*
>
> *Then Peter said, '***Silver or gold I do not have, but what I do have I give you. In the name of Jesus Christ of Nazareth, walk***.'* **Taking him by the right hand**, *he* **helped him up**, *and instantly the man's feet and ankles* **became strong**. *He jumped to his feet and began to walk. Then he* **went with** *them* **into the temple courts**, *walking and jumping,* **and praising God**. *When all the people saw him walking and praising God, they recognized him as the same man* **who used to sit begging** *at the temple gate called Beautiful, and they were* **filled with wonder and amazement** *at what had happened to him."* —Acts 3:1-10, emphasis added

The first thing I notice is that a sacred community does not have to be large to be powerful. In Acts 3 we read it was Peter and John who were involved. God does not need a large number of people to bring healing and salvation. All throughout Scripture we read stories where God brought victory, salvation, and healing through a small number of people who made themselves available.

"Now a man who was lame from birth was being carried to the temple gate called beautiful."

Did you notice the movement in the story? It begins with a man who is lame and ends with a man who is jumping around. We need to stop and think on the word "lame." Lame describes not only this man, but all of us since the fall. Our world is lame. We all know people and situations that are lame. We live in a lame world. That is just the way things are. However, this verse also contains great hope. My heart leaps when I read "*being carried to the temple gate called Beautiful.*" First, it leaps because I picture Jesus carrying my lame self to the gate called Beautiful. I may be lame now, but I will not remain this way. I am being healed. I will be beautiful again. Secondly, my heart leaps because I know so many other people whose lives are also lame. They have been broken, abused by sin and a world filled with evil. Yet I think about how sacred communities carry these lame people to something beautiful, and I get very excited. Our lives, our presence and our actions are a voice of hope in the world. We get to carry things that are lame to a gate called Beautiful! We get to participate in God's kingdom coming to earth.

"Peter looked him straight in the eye."

When was the last time you looked directly into the face of someone begging, someone terribly alone, or someone in desperate need of help? If we are going to live as the sacred community God has called us to be and bring heaven to earth, we must have "eyes that see" (Matthew 13:16). We must go through our normal day paying attention to what God is doing all around us. The Enemy will do his best to distract us. He will try to keep us too busy to notice the hurting person at lunch. He will attempt to keep us so preoccupied with our own pain and need to belong, that we fail to notice our teammate who is going through a hard time and in need of a friend to help them through it.

"Then Peter said, 'Silver or gold I do not have, but what I do have I give you. In the name of Jesus Christ of Nazareth, walk.'"

Peter and John did not have money. They did not have the resources this world says are important to having power and privilege. As far as this world is concerned they were poor and flat out broke. Yet, what they did have was true authentic raw power. They were operating in the power of God's Spirit. Over and over throughout God's story we read where God takes the things that are "weak" and uses them to show His strength. Perhaps you can relate to Peter and John. Perhaps you don't feel that you have what it takes. Maybe you wish you had more talent, or wished you looked differently? However, according to God's Word, what you possess does not matter near as much as if God possesses you. When I was in high school one simple statement motivated me to begin believing that perhaps God could use someone as ordinary as me. It is the statement, "It is not your ability that counts, but your availability." If you will open your eyes to the needs in our world and make yourself available to God, He will use you. He will supply the power and everything that is needed. Over the years I have learned that things like money, talent, and power only get in the way of us making ourselves available to God. I might even be suggesting that the less you have means the more God may be able to do with you. God told the apostle Paul, "*My grace is sufficient for you, for my power is made perfect in weakness*" (2 Corinthians 12:9). Where there is less of you, there is more room for Him.

"Taking him by the right hand, he helped him up, and instantly the man's feet and ankles became strong."

Noticing the lonely person at lunch or realizing there are people all around you who are "lame" is not enough. We must get involved. We must act in tangible ways, just like Jesus and His first followers did. In the same way that God put on a physical body so that He could take us by the hand and raise us up

(Ephesians 2:6), we now must take the hand of those who are lame so we can lift them up to something higher. In other words, being a sacred community used to bring heaven to earth is a costly endeavor. I know a young lady who noticed the poor and marginalized children living in Croc, Mexico. She felt like God was calling her to spend a week loving, playing with, and caring for the kids living there. The problem was the week her sacred community was going to Mexico was the same week as her cheerleading camp. If she was not at cheerleading camp, she would not be able to be on the cheerleading squad. In other words, the cost of going to Mexico was not being a varsity cheerleader her junior year in high school. However, the stronger reality was that if she was to go to the cheerleading camp she could not take the hands of her friends in Mexico and help them up.

God's healing power flowed through the body and out of the hand of Peter and the lame man became strong, able to walk and leap for joy. The same power, the same Spirit flowing through Peter, flows through you. When you choose to take others by the hand, know that God's power is active and working. He will strengthen the weak. He will raise up the lame. He is bringing heaven to earth.

The account of this story ends with Luke telling us **that the people were filled with wonder and amazement at what had happened to him.** Too many students I know are bored. They were made to be part of something bigger, but they don't know what it is. They crave adventure and long to take risks. It is like they know there has to be more to life than making good grades, hanging out on the weekends with friends and going to church on Sunday. They know it deep in their heart even if they don't have the words to explain it. I believe that ache in their heart is God calling them to risk their lives in His mission. How about you?

Have you ever been bored with your life? Do you ever long for something more? Have you ever sensed something was missing? Perhaps that void is God calling you, asking you to join Him in His mission. I dare you open your eyes and discover someone who is lame, then go take them by the hand and help them up. As you begin to sense God's healing power surge through you, take joy in knowing you are partnering with God. Be filled with wonder and amazement that God used you. Discover purpose as you realize God is using you to accomplish His work and mission in the world. What you do and the way you choose to live your life matters!

Act

Every time you include an outsider, every time you show compassion, every time you feed the hungry, visit the sick, or clean up the environment you are bringing heaven to earth. You are partnering with God in the healing of creation. Your community is a song and sample of heaven. Your very presence waifs in the air like a fragrant aroma of Jesus and His kingdom; when others around you catch a whiff, they will want to take a bite.

The church is "the people of God who are called and sent to represent the reign of God." **(*Missional Church,* p 15)**

Choose one of the following and do it. (Or respond to something else you may feel the Lord leading you to do.)

- Visit an elderly person you know (check with your parents or someone at your church if you don't know any) and ask them to tell you about their childhood. Listen to them, love them, and think about the fact that you are being Jesus to them.
- Organize a trip to a near by homeless shelter and feed the hungry and love the poor in Jesus' name.
- Buy ice cream sandwiches (if it is warm out) and walk around your neighborhood handing them out for free.
- Say hi to someone new at school who looks like they could use a friend.
- You and your friends who are reading this book have a "party" at your house and invite people from your school or neighborhood who typically don't get invited to parties.

Reflect

What activity did you choose to do yesterday?

How did it go?

What went well?

What will you do differently next time?

What questions do you have about "bringing heaven to earth"?

What are some of the biggest problems facing your community, school, or friends today?

What is your favorite verse, sentence, or word from Acts 3:1-10? Why?

THE
WAY OF
SHARING

Talk

Gather together into groups of 3-5 and take turns sharing your answers to the questions from the *Reflect* section. If most of the people in your group have not answered them yet, consider giving them a few minutes to do so before you start sharing.

After everyone has had a chance to share what they wrote down, take time to pray together. Consider going around the circle with everyone praying for the person who is on their left. Close your time of prayer by praying the Lord's Prayer together.

Transform

"Therefore, I urge you, brothers, in view of God's mercy, to offer your bodies as living sacrifices, holy and pleasing to God—this is your spiritual act of worship. Do not conform any longer to the pattern of this world, but be transformed by the renewing of your mind. Then you will be able to test and approve what God's will is—his good, pleasing and perfect will."

—Romans 12:1-2

As you take time today to consider your own transformation into greater Christ-likeness, take a moment to consider the amazing transformation that occurred in the life of Peter. Consider the ways Peter changed from Matthew 26 to Acts 3.

From Matthew 26:31-35, 69-75:

"Then Jesus told them, "This very night you will all fall away on account of me, for it is written: 'I will strike the shepherd, and the sheep of the flock will be scattered. But after I have risen, I will go ahead of you into Galilee.' Peter replied, 'Even if all fall away on account of you, I never will.' 'Truly I tell you,' Jesus answered, 'this very night, before the rooster crows, you will disown me three times.' But Peter declared, 'Even if I have to die with you, I will never disown you.' And all the other disciples said the same."

"Now Peter was sitting out in the courtyard, and a servant girl came to him. "You also were with Jesus of Galilee,' she said. But he denied it before them all. 'I don't know what you're talking about,' he said. Then he went out to the gateway, where another servant girl saw him and said to the people there, 'This fellow was with Jesus of Nazareth.' He denied it again, with an oath: 'I don't know the man!' After a little while, those standing there went up to Peter and said, 'Surely you are one of them; your accent gives you away.' Then he began to call down curses, and he swore to them, 'I don't know the man!' Immediately a

rooster crowed. Then Peter remembered the word Jesus had spoken: 'Before the rooster crows, you will disown me three times.' And he went outside and wept bitterly."

Make a list of 5 ways that Peter changed.

Make a list of 5 things you'd like to do differently as you consider how God may want to use you to "bring heaven to earth." When you are finished share them with a parent or a trusted friend.

Rest

"Be still, and know that I am God."
—Psalm 46:10

The phrase "be still" in Hebrew (the language used to write most of the Old Testament) is "rapha." Rapha is also translated as "sink down" in Isaiah 5:24 (NIV). "*Therefore, as tongues of fire lick up straw and as dry grass sinks down in the flames.*" Another way to think about what it means to "be still" is to think about "sinking down" into God, like grass into a flame.

How are you feeling today? Are you tired or stressed out? If so, I want to encourage you to "sink down" into God and lose your life in Him, like dry grass in a flame. Quit trying to control and manage your life today and simply rest in God's love for you. Allow yourself to sink down deeper into God's love. As the apostle John put it, "Be loved today."

The NRSV translates the word "rapha" with the word "collapse." Maybe it is helpful for you to imagine yourself collapsing into God's arms of love like you would collapse into your bed when it is very late and you're so tired you cannot stand up any longer. (Perhaps you are physically tired and need to physically collapse into your bed and get some much-needed rest.)

Preview

The word *community* has many connotations—some positive and some negative. Community can make us think of a safe togetherness, shared meals, common goals, and joyful celebrations. It also can call forth images of exclusiveness, in-group language, and self-satisfied isolation. However, community is first of all a quality of the heart. It grows from the spiritual knowledge that we are alive; not for ourselves, but for one another. Community is the fruit of our capacity to make the interests of others more important than our own (see Philippians 2:4). The question is not "How can we make community?" but "How can we develop and nurture giving hearts?"

In a world so torn apart by rivalry, anger, and hatred, we have the privileged vocation to be living signs of a love that can bridge all divisions and heal all wounds. —Henri Nouwen

"Love from the center of who you are; don't fake it.
Run for dear life from evil; hold on for dear life to good.
Be good friends who love deeply;
practice playing second fiddle."
—Romans 12:9,10, MSG

"John answered, 'Anyone who has two shirts should share with the one who has none, and anyone who has food should do the same.'"
—Luke 3:11, TNIV

"By this everyone will know that you are my disciples,
if you love one another."
—John 13:35

Clearly one of the most obvious marks of the early church was sharing. They willingly shared their stuff with one another rather than holding on to it. What makes this even more astounding is the fact that the disciples were very different from one another. They didn't all see things the same way. They often disagreed with each other and I am sure annoyed each other from time to time. In other words, the love they expressed to one another ran much deeper than common interests. Their love for one another was rooted in the love of God they witnessed for themselves in Jesus' death on the Cross. They could love one another like family because they all saw Jesus as their brother and God as their father.

Let's examine the make up of Jesus' disciples and I think we will quickly discover that it was more than playing on the same baseball team in the summer or having similar play lists on their ipods that led them to share everything with one another.

The gospel writers were careful to give us the names of Jesus' 12 disciples and, in some cases, a little bit of background on them. (See Mark 3:13-19, Matthew 10:2-4 and Luke 6:14-16.) By reading through these descriptive lists we quickly learn that at least two of the 12 disciples belonged to the "Zealots." The Zealots were an angry group of people who hated the Romans. The Romans had taken over the land of Israel and their very presence polluted the land and was seen as a huge hindrance to worshiping God. The Zealots were in favor of using force to defeat the hated Romans. Not only did the Zealots despise the Romans, they did not have much love for anyone who tolerated the Romans. In other words "if you are a friend of Rome you are no friend of mine" was their attitude. Simon and Judas Iscariot more than likely both belonged to the Zealots.

What makes this so interesting is that not only did Jesus pick a couple Zealots to be in His inner circle, He also chose the likes of Matthew. What do you we know about Matthew's occupation? Both Matthew and Luke are careful to point out that he was a tax collector. Why do they do this? Why is it important? One reason is what it teaches us what Jesus had in mind when He talked about community, sharing, and getting along with one another.

So what's the big deal? Tax collectors worked closely with the Romans. They collected taxes on behalf of the wealthy Romans who were occupying the land, making life very hard for the Jews. Not only that, these tax collectors were allowed to charge a little extra from their fellow Jews in order to get rich themselves. In other words, the tax collectors were partners of sorts with the Romans. Can you see the problem here? Jesus called together people who did not like each other, in fact they could have been enemies. Yet they came to love each other so dearly that instead of killing each other, they died for each other. Now that's transformation. They had seen love modeled and taught by Jesus. Jesus taught a different way to live. He modeled and taught a way of self-sacrifice and radical love.

> *"By this all men will know you are my disciples, if you love one another."*
> —John 13:35

> *"Greater love has no one than this, than he lay down his life for his friends."*
> —John 15:13

This collection of people became so close none of them held on to their own possessions like it belonged to them. Acts tells us they opened up their hands and willingly gave all they had to anyone in the group who might need what they had. Why? They gave freely because they had pledged allegiance to Jesus and living His way. They saw Jesus lay down His very life for them and they were committed to doing the same. In order to love Jesus, they understood they must love one another in the same radical ways. They understood their calling was to love one another in such radical and tangible ways that the rest of the world would take notice and recognize them as having been with Jesus (Acts 4:13).

One of the clear marks of the early church was unity. Luke records in Acts 4:32 that *"All believers were one in heart and mind. No one claimed that any of their possessions was their own, but they shared everything they had."*

This unity and commonality is so different from the culture most of us live in. Most of us live in a culture that is marked more by individualism and selfishness. A youth group is content to be a loose collection of individuals. A sacred community is *one* body with many members. This week we want to explore the difference together.

Meditate

As you read today's text, keep in mind that God's story is meant to be lived and not to be read and forgotten. As you read, think about ways you may be able to reenact this powerful story in your own life.

> *"All the believers were one in heart and mind. No one claimed that any of their possessions was their own, but they shared everything they had. With great power the apostles continued to testify to the resurrection of the Lord Jesus. And God's grace was so powerfully at work in them all that there were no needy persons among them. For from time to time those who owned land or houses sold them, brought the money from the sales and put it at the apostles' feet, and it was distributed to anyone who had need. Joseph, a Levite from Cyprus, whom the apostles called Barnabas (which means "son of encouragement"), sold a field he owned and brought the money and put it at the apostles' feet."*
>
> —Acts 4:32-37

There is tremendous unity and togetherness in a sacred community that is often missing in a youth group. A sacred community is bound together by the love of Jesus Christ through the power of the Holy Spirit. A shared love for Jesus Christ knits their hearts together, weaving their lives into one fabric.

Youth groups on the other hand often have nothing more than fickle common interests holding people together. Rather than being united by a sincere love for God, one another, and the world, they are divided by a selfish love for themselves.

If you remember a few chapters back we talked about how the way of prayer is an essential ingredient and mark of being a sacred community. I would even go so far as to say that if your community is not learning how to pray (I mean wait upon the Lord in order to receive all that He is and has for you), your community will not be able to live the way of sharing. Let me see if I can explain. I think there is an order, or sequence, that needs to be followed. We can see this order throughout Scripture in both the OT and the NT. One of the places it is very clear is in Jesus' teaching in John 15 about the Vine and the branches. Jesus points out that in order for a branch to do what it was created to do (bear fruit) it must remain, abide, or stay connected to the vine. When the branch becomes severed or separated in any way from the vine, it begins to die and can produce nothing and is good for nothing. Jesus says He is the Vine and we are the branches. Our number one priority is to remain, abide, or stay connected to Jesus. He is the source. From Him flows life, love, and all that we need to be fully alive. Therefore, before we do anything else we must learn to pray. We must learn how to stay connected to Him. The branch that remains connected to the Vine will flourish by producing much fruit. The branch that becomes separated from the Vine will shrivel up and die.

Now let's see what this has to do with loving one another and sharing. Those who remain in Jesus, receive from Jesus the love of God. As they remain in Jesus, this love continues to flow, filling up their hearts and minds, healing them and making them whole. They are constantly reminded of who they are, the much loved children of God (Galatians 4 and Romans 8). Because they have received love, they are now able to love others. Because they have an abundance of love filling up and overflowing in their own hearts and lives, they can share that love with others they meet. Perhaps you can imagine love flowing from God, into their hearts and then overflowing from their hearts until it spills out into the hearts and lives of other people (friends and family) around them. John puts it this way in one of his letters, "*We love because he first loved us.*" In other words our ability to love one another is dependent upon our ability to first be loved by God. In the same letter he wrote, "*Beloved let us love one another.*" Look closer at the word "beloved" and you can make a command out of it, the command is to be loved. I believe that is God's first and primary command to each one of us. Be loved. Once we do that, we can then love one another. Once a person has come to know and believe the love that God has for them, they are then free to love others people around them.

On the other hand, a person who has not come to experience and know God's love working powerfully in them is not free to love others. Because they don't know and believe that they are already loved, they will use other people in order to try and discover love. They are slaves to other people's opinions and ideas about them.

When we fail to understand and experience the love God has for us, more emphasis gets placed on being with people who share my interests. The desire to be with people who share my interests begins to override the commonality we all share through the Holy Spirit. When this happens cliques begin to develop based on these common interests. The athletes begin to sit with other athletes, the band members only hang out with other band members, and the pretty and the popular circle the wagons making it tough for others to join in. Sure they still may gather on the same night and in the same room for "youth group," but they are not of "*one heart and mind*" (Philippians 2). They are divided and therefore they are weak. Power comes from unity and from the ability to lay aside oneself for the good of the group. This weakness becomes more obvious when you see what happens when you see the students relating to each other outside of the youth group meeting. For example, when the students are at school or the mall, and there is no youth room forcing them together, do they still gravitate toward one another? Do they find themselves being drawn toward one another by love and the power of the Holy Spirit?

Act

Take one minute to recognize God being present with you as you read.

Read through Acts 4:32-37 out loud so you can hear the words with your own ears.

Now read through the text silently, underlining all the words that stand out to you.

Now begin to think and brainstorm things your sacred community could share. See if you cannot come up with at least 10 ideas. Do not worry or try to figure out if they are good ideas or if they would work or not. Just write down as many ideas as you can think of.

Reflect

Read Acts 4:32-37.

Where have you seen communities of people who willingly sacrifice for one another? Here are some categories to help you think.

Movies (if a clip from a movie comes to mind, consider showing the clip when you gather to talk with your group)
Books
TV
Sports Teams
Families you know
Clubs
Performing arts groups

How did sharing with one another look in the groups of people you thought of?

What community have you been a part of that is most like the community described in Acts 4:32-37?

Look over your brainstorming list from yesterday and add any additional ideas that have come to your mind.

Circle your five favorite ideas. Be prepared to share these along with your other ideas if necessary when you get together with your group tomorrow.

THE WAY
OF INCLUDING

Talk

Gather together with your group and share examples of where you've seen communities of people making sacrifices for one another. If someone has a good video clip to share, show it.

Have someone read Acts 4:32-37 so everyone can hear it.

Take turns sharing what words or phrases stand out. People should also share why it is meaningful to them.

Have people share their list of ideas for how the sacred community could share with one another. Depending on the size of your group, you may want to have everyone share all their ideas or just start with their five favorites. Select someone to write down the ideas, preferably where everyone can see them.

Once you have a good list, begin to discuss which ideas are the favorites of the group. Pray and ask God to lead your group in picking at least one thing your group could begin sharing.

If possible, select one thing the group will begin to "have in common" and share with one another. Write that one thing here.

Have everyone gather together in a circle, consider holding hands or linking arms as you pray the Lord's Prayer together.

May the peace of the Lord Christ go with you,
wherever He may send you.
May He guide you through the wilderness,
protect you through the storm.
May He bring you home rejoicing
at the wonders He has shown you.
May He bring you home rejoicing
once again into our doors.

—Benediction from the Northumbria Community

You might consider closing with this benediction from the Northumbria Community in England.

Transform

What has been your favorite part of going through this journal this past week?

What was the worst part about it?

Where have you seen God at work in or around you over the past seven days?

What is one thing that is really hard for you to share? Why is that?

Consider the following prayer by Jim Elliot.

Father, Let me be weak that I might loose my clutch on everything temporary, My life, my reputation, my possessions, Lord, let me loose the tension of the grasping hand. Even, Father, would I lose the love of fondling. How often I have released a grasp only to retain what I prized by "harmless" longing, the fondling touch. Rather open my hand to receive the nail of Calvary, as Christ's was opened—that I, releasing all, might be released, unleashed from all that binds me now.

Rest

"Be still, and know that I am God."
—Psalm 46:10

Quit trying so hard today and simply know that God loves you.

O abyss, O eternal Godhead, O sea profound, what more could you give me than yourself? You are the fire that burns without being consumed; you consume in your heat all the soul's self-love; you are the fire which takes away cold; with your light you illuminate me so that I may know all your truth. Clothe me, clothe me with yourself, eternal truth, so that I may run this mortal life with true obedience, and with the light of your most holy faith. —Catherine of Siena (1347-1380)

Preview

"When he saw the crowds, he had compassion on them, because they were harassed and helpless, like sheep without a shepherd."
—Matthew 9:36

And so he said, "Blessed are the spiritual zeros-the spiritually bankrupt, deprived and deficient, the spiritual beggars, those without a wisp of religion-when the kingdom of heaven comes upon them."
(Dallas Willard paraphrasing Jesus in *The Divine Conspiracy,* p 100)

Jesus used parties and eating with others as an opportunity to demonstrate what life was like in God's kingdom. In God's kingdom there are no outsiders. The love of God is expansive, compelling, and inclusive. When you share a meal with Jesus you quickly learn that there are no strangers, sinners, or outsiders. Read Matthew 9:10-13 if you want to see for yourself what I'm trying to say.

I want you to consider right now your commitment to follow Jesus. I believe following Jesus at school will take you to tables where you would not normally sit and more importantly to people who you would not normally eat with. You also need to understand that if you choose to disrupt the status quo, you will mess with people's minds and the neat categories they have created. People typically do not like that. Just as the Pharisees did not understand what Jesus was up to, many will not understand what you are up to (unless they understand what it means to live the way of Jesus).

Think about the words of Jesus, *"I desire mercy, not sacrifice."*

As we continue to follow and learn from some of Jesus' earliest followers we quickly understand that they also tore down walls and invited "strangers" and "enemies" to be part of their sacred community. In Acts 2:47 we read that the early church community was *"enjoying the favor of all the people."* It appears that this community of believers lived in such a way among other people, that those not yet part of the community really wanted to become a part. In other words, the early church community enjoyed a great reputation among the common normal people of the day, even if the religious leaders wanted to kill them.

What is the reputation of your church community at school? Are you seen as more including or excluding of others? How inviting is your group? If the students at your school were asked to use one word to describe your church community, what do you think some of the words would be? What are some words you hope would be used?

Meditate

Grab your Bible and open up to Acts 10 and carefully read the whole chapter.

Cornelius was a Gentile. He was an outsider. Jews, like Peter, who wanted to love and worship God were not permitted to have fellowship (eat) with Gentiles without becoming "unclean." Are there people in your school or neighborhood that others have labeled as "a bad kid?"

Notice that even though Jews had a problem conversing and relating to Cornelius, God apparently had no such problem.

Peter's vision was about Peter learning that God was making all people clean through Jesus Christ (Acts 10:34-36). No longer should Peter, or anyone else, label a person unclean or an outsider. Anyone who wants to come to Jesus should be encouraged to do so. The healing power of the Cross is more potent than the destructive power of sin. Jews should no longer fear hanging out with Gentiles. All people are equally loved and accepted by God through Jesus Christ. What is one group of people who come closest to being like the Gentiles in the Book of Acts?

How do you think Peter felt, going to hang out at Cornelius's house? How would you have felt? Why did he do it? Think of a group at students that you would classify as "outsiders" according to the people you typically hang out with. How would you feel going over to one of their houses to hang out with them on the weekend? Why would you ever do something like that?

Notice that love and holiness is more powerful than hatred and sin. It is the same with light and darkness. Darkness is no match for light. When the sun rises each new day, the night is over. When Jesus hung out with "sinners," they became whole.

What action or sign, according to Acts 10:44-48, confirmed that the Gentiles had been accepted by God and were now apart of the new family God was creating?

Act

"What good is it, my brothers, if a man claims to have faith but has no deeds? Can such faith save him? Suppose a brother or sister is without clothes and daily food. If one of you says to him, "Go, I wish you well; keep warm and well fed," but does nothing about his physical needs, what good is it? In the same way, faith by itself, if it is not accompanied by action, is dead." —James 2: 14-17

Option 1

Tomorrow (or sometime this week) when you walk into the lunchroom try to notice who is sitting with who. Notice the groupings. Do people tend to sit with people who are like them or different from them? Notice their clothing, hairstyles, mannerisms, speech, and other things you can pick up.

Option 2

With at least one or two other friends look for someone, or a couple people, who are sitting alone at lunch and invite them to come and eat with you (or ask if you can sit with them).

Reflect

Do you sense there being any tension between seeking to love God and living a holy life on one hand and being friends with others who may be far from God or want nothing to do with Him? How did Jesus handle this tension?

If you were giving advice to another Christian about loving and including people who are "outsiders," what would you say?

How did your experience in the lunchroom go?

What did you learn about yourself?

What did you learn about others?

Is there a next step you should take to continue living as Jesus would have you live at your school? What might it be?

Where did you see signs that God was at work?

THE WAY OF SUFFERING AND PERSECUTION

"Blessed are those who are persecuted because of righteousness, for theirs is the kingdom of heaven."
—Matthew 5:10

"After his suffering, he (Jesus) showed himself to these men and gave many convincing proofs that he was alive . . ."
—Acts 1:3

Keep in mind that being a witness for Jesus is not really something you do on your own. It is something you do in the context of a larger community. You alone are not the body of Christ. You as part of your sacred community are the body of Christ. We really do need each other!

Prayer for Mission

Lord Jesus Christ, you stretched out your arms of love on the hard wood of the cross that everyone might come within the reach of your saving embrace: So clothe us in your Spirit that we, reaching forth our hands in love, may bring those who do not know you to the knowledge and love of you; for the honor of your Name. ***Amen.***

***(The Book of Common Prayer,* p 101)**

Talk

Get into groups of 3-4 and share what you wrote down yesterday in the *Reflect* section.

Close by praying the "Prayer for Mission" from the *Book of Common Prayer* from yesterday's reflection.

Transform

Spiritual formation takes time. In our fast food, texting, instant messaging, and microwave world, waiting can be very hard. Even though a person may cram for a test, one cannot cram for spiritual formation. Just as it takes about 9 months for a healthy baby to be born after conception—there is nothing you can do to speed that up. It takes time for the "new you" to be birthed.

God is transforming you into Christ's likeness, but it will take time. Be patient, wait, and trust.

> *"He who began a good work in you will carry it on to completion until the day of Christ Jesus."* —Philippians 1:6

Think back over the past week and what you've read, done, and talked about with your friends. What stands out to you now about becoming more inclusive like Jesus and the early church?

Can you think of any instances from this past week where you were more inviting than you have been in the past?

If you were to give yourself a grade on how you were at welcoming and including outsiders, what grade would you give yourself? What grade would you have given yourself a year ago?

What is one thing you can do in partnership with God who is making you into a more compassionate, welcoming, and inclusive person?

Rest

"Be still, and know that I am God."
—Psalm 46:10

"My heart is not proud, O Lord,
my eyes are not haughty;
I do not concern myself with great matters
or things too wonderful for me.

But I have stilled and quieted my soul;
like a weaned child with its mother,
like a weaned child is my soul within me.

O Israel, put your hope in the Lord
both now and forevermore."

—Psalm 131:1-3

Take time today to crawl up into the arms of God and rest.

Preview

Have you noticed there are some rules you are supposed to follow in order to get where you want to go today? These rules, or ways of living, can often times go in the opposite direction from what Jesus taught.

For example: A slogan by a fast food company was simply, “Have it your way.” That is a philosophy, or way of life, that is very popular today. It says, think of yourself first. Yet, that goes in the opposite direction of Jesus’ teaching to think of others first.

I know today it is very popular to talk with our friends about another person’s drama or problems. Or if a friend offends us, the “normal” thing to do is to talk with another friend about it. Jesus teaches us that we should not talk about the person who has offended us. However, if we feel we need to talk about it, we should go directly to the person.

This is where it gets difficult. I have seen students up close who have refused to play the gossip game or to make fun of fellow classmates and they ended up being the ones left out. For whatever reason, the students doing the “normal and popular” things turned on the ones trying to live a different way (the way of Jesus).

None of us should be surprised when we are misunderstood, left out, or feel hated on account of Jesus. Listen to what Jesus had to say on this very subject.

> *“If the world hates you, keep in mind that it hated me first. If you belonged to the world, it would love you as its own. As it is, you do not belong to the world, but I have chosen you out of the world. That is why the world hates you. Remember the words I spoke to you: ‘No servant is greater than his master.’ If they persecuted me, they will persecute you also.”*
>
> —John 15:18

If you are committed to following Jesus, then prepare yourself to feel left out. Going the way of Jesus is going to take you "against the flow" of what is normal and popular today. As followers of Jesus we don't want to be hated because we are judgmental and mean. We also don't want to be rejected because we don't know how to have fun with normal people. Neither of those two ways is Christian. However, if loving Jesus and loving others causes us to stand out, then so be it. We must not compromise our faith and practices just so we fit in with a group of people who have it wrong. Staying faithful to Jesus, even when it means being alone, can be the most difficult thing you will have to do. Perhaps it will help to remind yourself that you are not alone and that the reason you feel you are alone is because the rest of the world is traveling the wrong way down the one-way street (not you, and eventually everyone will figure that out, so just hang in there).

Meditate

All throughout the life of Jesus and the early church we see examples of suffering and persecution. We are going to focus on one story found in Acts 4:1-22. Grab your Bible and open up to the text. Use the following prayer to prepare your heart to hear from God.

> **I would be silent, now,**
> **Lord,**
> **and expectant . . .**
> **that I may receive the gift I need,**
> **so I may become the gift others need.**
> **(Ted Loder, *Guerrillas of Grace*)**

Slowly read through the text twice, out loud if you can at least once.

> *"The priests and the captain of the temple guard and the Sadducees came up to Peter and John while they were speaking to the people. They were greatly disturbed because the apostles were teaching the people and proclaiming in Jesus the resurrection of the dead. They seized Peter and John, and because it was evening, they put them in jail until the next day. But many who heard the message believed, and the number of men grew to about five thousand.*
>
> *The next day the rulers, elders and teachers of the law met in Jerusalem. Annas the high priest was there, and so were Caiaphas, John, Alexander and the other men of the high priest's family. They had Peter and John brought before them and began to question them: 'By what power or what name did you do this?'*
>
> *Then Peter, filled with the Holy Spirit, said to them: 'Rulers and elders of the people! If we are being called to account today for an act of kindness shown to a cripple and are asked how he was healed, then know this, you and all the people of Israel: It is by the name of Jesus Christ of Nazareth, whom you crucified but whom God raised from the dead, that this*

man stands before you healed. He is the stone you builders rejected, which has become the capstone, Salvation is found in no one else, for there is no other name under heaven given to men by which we must be saved.'

When they saw the courage of Peter and John and realized that they were unschooled, ordinary men, they were astonished and they took note that these men had been with Jesus. But since they could see the man who had been healed standing there with them, there was nothing they could say. So they ordered them to withdraw from the Sanhedrin and then conferred together. 'What are we going to do with these men?' they asked. 'Everybody living in Jerusalem knows they have done an outstanding miracle, and we cannot deny it. But to stop this thing from spreading any further among the people, we must warn these men to speak no longer to anyone in this name.'

Then they called them in again and commanded them not to speak or teach at all in the name of Jesus. But Peter and John replied, 'Judge for yourselves whether it is right in God's sight to obey you rather than God. For we cannot help speaking about what we have seen and heard.'

After further threats they let them go. They could not decide how to punish them, because all the people were praising God for what had happened. For the man who was miraculously healed was over forty years old.

—Acts 4:1-22

Why are the Sadducees so upset with Peter and John? (verse 2)

What are some things that Christian students may do today that would disturb or upset others not following Jesus?

Have you ever felt persecuted, misunderstood, or left out because of trying to follow Jesus? What was that like? How did it feel?

Typically, Christian students in America are not thrown in jail for following Jesus. How might persecution and suffering look today for students following Jesus?

Verse 11 is quoting Psalm 118:22, and says, "*the stone you builders rejected, which has become the capstone.*" In other words, popular wisdom threw Jesus out the window. Yet, Jesus becomes the very cornerstone upon which God builds His entire Kingdom.

Is it helpful to realize that even though you may be rejected (like Jesus was) now, God will use you and your faithfulness to continue building and expanding His kingdom on earth right where you live.

Remaining faithful and strong while being persecuted is hard and requires great strength. As you read Acts 4:13 again, consider where Peter and John found such courage. Where do you think such bold courage came from?

Do you imagine God could grant you the same strength, boldness, and courage? Why not ask Him for it right now? Consider writing out your prayer below.

Peter and John refused to be quiet about the things they had seen Jesus do. Why do you think they refused to be silent?

What have you seen and heard about Jesus that you can tell to others?

How do you imagine God feels when He hears His children talking out loud about the great things He has done?

Why do you think the Enemy tries so hard to shut up Christians from telling the great stories about what God has done for His people?

What else strikes you about this story?

Consider using the following prayer as you wrap up this time with God.

> ***Almighty and everlasting God, as you gave great boldness and courage to John and Peter, grant us today the same courage that we may boldly tell of the great things you are doing today. Help us to endure when we are called upon to suffer for You. Free us from the pursuit of comfort and security that we may take the risks that following you calls for. We remember your followers around the world who suffer much more than we do for your name. Provide food for those who are hungry, comfort to those who are alone, strength to those being tortured and do it all for the sake of Jesus who lived and died for us and who now lives and reigns with you and the Holy Spirit, one God, forever and ever. Amen.***

Act

Perhaps you are already aware that many Christians actually **choose** to suffer for the sake of Jesus. Consider these words from the apostle Paul.

> *"So do not be ashamed to testify about our Lord, or ashamed of me his prisoner. But* ***join with me in suffering*** *for the gospel, by the power of God."* —2 Timothy 1:8, emphasis added

> *"That is why I am* ***suffering*** *as I am. Yet I am not ashamed, because I know whom I have believed, and am convinced that he is able to guard what I have entrusted to him for that day."*
> —2 Timothy 1:12, emphasis added

> *"This is my gospel, for which I am* ***suffering*** *even to the point of being chained like a criminal. But God's word is not chained."*
> —2 Timothy 2:9, emphasis added

> *"For just as* ***the sufferings of Christ flow over into our lives****, so also through Christ our comfort overflows."*
> —2 Corinthians 1:5, emphasis added

While there are many reasons Christians have chosen to suffer for Jesus, consider this list.

1. Because Jesus himself suffered and to choose Jesus is to choose to suffer. The way of Jesus has always been the way of the Cross.

2. To demonstrate that real satisfaction and comfort come only from Jesus.

3. In order to join in the work of Christ in the world.

4. We show the value of Christ in our lives by what we are willing to sacrifice in order to have Him.

What reasons for suffering would you add to the list?

5.

Pick from the list below or come up with you own idea of how you could choose to "suffer for the gospel."

- Stop buying drinks for a month and put that money aside to help provide clean drinking water for those who don't have it.
- Get up 30 minutes early every day for the next week in order to spend time with Jesus in the Word and in prayer.
- Take the back seat when getting in the car with friends or family.
- Choose the longest check-out line at the store.
- Volunteer to watch the kids of a family so the parents can have a night out.
- Clean the toilets in your house without telling anyone about it.
- Give $20 to someone who needs it more than you do.
- Figure out how to be a friend to someone who is lonely.
- Fast from watching TV, going online, texting, or something else you'd really miss and use that time to consider how strong your desire for Jesus is.

Reflect

Think back (or look in your journal) on the different scriptures we've looked at this week. Which one is the most meaningful to you? Write it out in the space below.

Why do feel this particular scripture is important? Why is it meaningful to you?

You should have selected your "Choosing to suffer" activity by now from the *Act* section. Write more about it below.

What are you doing? ________________________________

How long will it last? ________________________________

Why will it be hard? ________________________________

Why are you doing it? ________________________________

How are you feeling about your task? ________________________

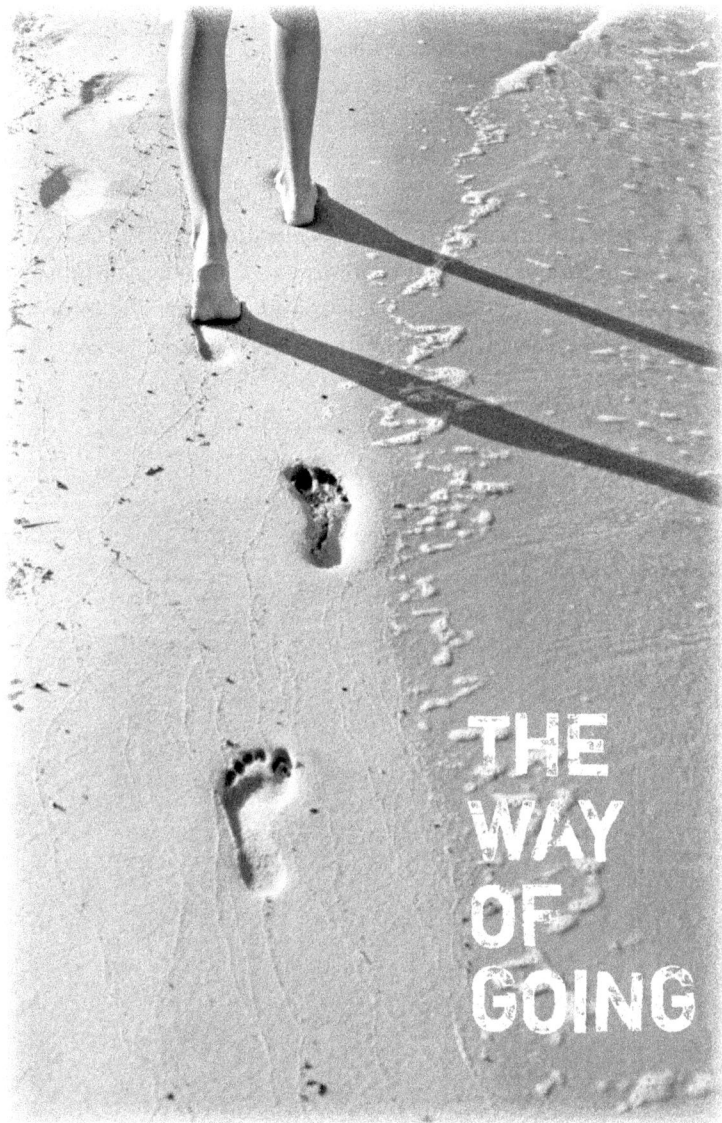

THE WAY OF GOING

Talk

Go around the group and allow each person to share what scripture from the week has been especially meaningful and why.

Give everyone a chance to share how they will choose to suffer during the next week. Everyone should be able to use what they put down in the *Reflect* section as an outline for their sharing.

Pray for one another and the persecuted church. Consider using www.persecution.com to inform and inspire your prayers. The site has statistics, stories, videos and other helpful information about the persecuted church around the world today.

Transform

Think about the apostle Paul for a few minutes. He went from being the one **who persecuted** to being the one who **was persecuted**. Now that is quite a transformation.

Notice the striking difference in these two accounts of different times in Paul's life. The first is before he became a disciple of Jesus, the second one is after he began following Jesus.

> *"Then Paul said: 'I am a Jew, born in Tarsus of Cilicia, but brought up in this city. Under Gamaliel I was thoroughly trained in the law of our fathers and was just as zealous for God as any of you are today. I persecuted the followers of this Way to their death, arresting both men and women and throwing them into prison, as also the high priest and all the Council can testify. I even obtained letters from them to their brothers in Damascus, and went there to bring these people as prisoners to Jerusalem to be punished.'"* —Acts 22:3-5

> *"To this very hour we go hungry and thirsty, we are in rags, we are brutally treated, we are homeless. We work hard with our own hands. When we are cursed, we bless; when we are persecuted, we endure it; when we are slandered, we answer kindly. Up to this moment we have become the scum of the earth, the refuse of the world."* —1 Corinthians 4:11-13

It was to the Corinthians he wrote, *"Therefore, if anyone is in Christ, he is a new creation; the old has gone, the new has come"* (2 Corinthians 5:17).

It is quite obvious Paul became a new person. By the grace of God he was changed and transformed.

Suffering is one of the key instruments God uses to change us. What is the hardest thing you have suffered in your life?

What did you learn by going through that experience?

Are you able to see now how you became a better person by going through that experience? If so, how?

What has suffering taught you about yourself? (Think about the activity you chose or something else you have had to suffer through.)

Rest

"By the seventh day God had finished the work he had been doing; so on the seventh day he rested from all his work. And God blessed the seventh day and made it holy, because on it he rested from all the work of creating that he had done." —Genesis 2:2-4

"Six days you are to gather it, but on the seventh day, the Sabbath, there will not be any." —Exodus 16:26

"So the people rested on the seventh day." —Exodus 16:30

"For in six days the LORD made the heavens and the earth, the sea, and all that is in them, but he rested on the seventh day. Therefore the LORD blessed the Sabbath day and made it holy." —Exodus 20:11

"There are six days when you may work, but the seventh day is a Sabbath of rest, a day of sacred assembly. You are not to do any work; wherever you live, it is a Sabbath to the LORD." —Leviticus 23: 3

"And yet his work has been finished since the creation of the world. For somewhere he has spoken about the seventh day in these words: And on the seventh day God rested from all his work." —Hebrews 4:4

Go Rest.

Preview

A sending God and a sent people

God is missional. God is going and sending. God is love. This love is explosive and limitless with no bounds to contain or stop it. We read in John 3:16 that God loved the world so much that He sent His Son into the world to save it. Later, the Father and the Son sent the Spirit. Now this sending has grown to include the Father, Son and Holy Spirit sending the Church into the world. This concept of sending has been captured by the Latin phrase "mission Dei," which means "sent God" or "God who sends." The role of the Church, the people of God, is to join God in His missionary activity in the world. God has sent and is sending you and me into the world as His agents of restoration.

Fishers of men or keepers of the aquarium?

Just as Jesus was sent to seek and to save the lost, so the Church has been sent to seek and to save the lost. In the Gospels Jesus said, *"Follow me and I will make you fishers of men."* We have been called to cast our nets out in the wide open spaces where people gather. The nets we cast are our relationships with one another. Our community of love attracts and invites others to join. We have been called to participate in the breaking-in of God's kingdom all around us. However, instead of going fishing, many churches have settled for the far safer and self-serving role of cleaning the aquarium. Most churches do well at gathering together on Sunday morning, but do very poorly at going out and fishing for lost and broken people throughout the week. I think we must ask ourselves if we are "fishers of people" or only "keepers of the aquarium?"

Salt and Light

In Matthew 5 Jesus likened His community of followers to "salt" and "light." The thing about salt is that it does no good in the saltshaker. It brings out flavor only when it is poured out onto the food. Far too many churches are locked up in the saltshaker and are doing very little to represent Jesus in the neighborhoods where they are needed. What about light? Jesus says no one lights a candle and then sticks it under a bucket. He encourages us to let our light shine in the midst of those around us in such a way as they see our good works and know that God must be alive and active as well. But once again, far too many church communities are content to curse the darkness rather than penetrate it with the light of God's Presence shining in them.

Go and make disciples

Among Jesus' last words to His disciples (those who later formed what we now call the church) was, "***Go*** *and make disciples* . . . " Jesus did not wait or expect lost, hurting and sick people to find him. He went to them. Apparently Jesus did not want His disciples to stay locked up in a room or building either. He sent them out in the midst of the real world where the lost and broken are. Eugene Peterson argues that the way of Jesus is always local and ordinary. We read in Acts how the Church was sent from Jerusalem to Samaria and Judea and to the remotest parts of the earth.

The Holy Spirit has been sent by the Father and Son. The Holy Spirit is looking for people who will embody and proclaim the good news of Jesus Christ. If you are a Christian, then you are a missionary. You are being sent by God into a broken and often hostile world. Each of us individually, and more importantly collectively, are called to represent Jesus in the real and normal world where we live. We are His body.

If Jesus were to show up today and say to you, "Come follow me" where would He take you? Who would He go visit? What people would He be looking for? How would He spend His day? **Would you go** or would you stay?

Meditate

"Oh, how I love your law! I ***meditate*** *on it all day long."*
—Ps. 119:97, emphasis added

With every morn my life afresh must break
The crust of self, gathered about me fresh;
That thy wind-spirit may rush in and shake
The darkness out of me, and rend the mesh
The spider-devils spin out of the flesh-
Eager to net the soul before it wake,
That it may slumberous lie, and listen to the snake.
(C. S. Lewis, *Diary of an Old Soul*)

Take a couple deep breaths. As you breathe imagine the presence of God filling your entire body from head to toe. As you exhale, imagine all the darkness and junk you wish to be rid of leaving your body. Thank God for being with you this day; keeping in mind that reading the Bible is not just something you do, it is a person you are with.

Read through the text twice. Once out loud if you can (it might be strange to read out loud if sitting in the middle of class waiting for the bell to ring).

"Now an angel of the Lord said to Philip, 'Go south to the road—the desert road—that goes down from Jerusalem to Gaza.' So he started out, and on his way he met an Ethiopian eunuch, an important official in charge of all the treasury of Candace, queen of the Ethiopians. This man had gone to Jerusalem to worship, and on his way home was sitting in his chariot reading the book of Isaiah the prophet. The Spirit told Philip, 'Go to that chariot and stay near it.'

Then Philip ran up to the chariot and heard the man reading Isaiah the prophet. 'Do you understand what you are reading?' Philip asked.

'How can I,' he said, 'unless someone explains it to me?' So he invited Philip to come up and sit with him.

The eunuch was reading this passage of Scripture:

'He was led like a sheep to the slaughter,
and as a lamb before the shearer is silent,
so he did not open his mouth.
In his humiliation he was deprived of justice.
Who can speak of his descendants?
For his life was taken from the earth.'

The eunuch asked Philip, 'Tell me, please, who is the prophet talking about, himself or someone else?' Then Philip began with that very passage of Scripture and told him the good news about Jesus.

As they traveled along the road, they came to some water and the eunuch said, 'Look, here is water. Why shouldn't I be baptized?' And he gave orders to stop the chariot. Then both Philip and the eunuch went down into the water and Philip baptized him. When they came up out of the water, the Spirit of the Lord suddenly took Philip away, and the eunuch did not see him again, but went on his way rejoicing. Philip, however, appeared at Azotus and traveled about, preaching the gospel in all the towns until he reached Caesarea." —Acts 4:26-40

Use these questions to help you meditate on this story and work it into your life (or should I say work your life into the story).

List all the characters in the story

- An angel of the Lord

List all the verbs (action words)

- Go

Make a list of at least 10 observations from this story.

- An angel of the Lord sent Phillip south to the road.
-
-
-
-
-
-
-
-
-

If this scene were a movie, what title would you give it?

How can you apply this story to your life? Is there something God is speaking to you about from this text?

What is the Lord leading you to do in response to what you have read and understood from the story?

Act

"Do not let this Book of the Law depart from your mouth; meditate on it day and night, so that you may be careful to do everything written in it. Then you will be prosperous and successful."

—Joshua 1:8

Begin by reading again Acts 8:26-40 and going over your reflections from the questions.

Now that you've spent time meditating on God's Word, how will you do what it says? How will you join God in the work He is already doing? What is God prompting you to do?

Here are some suggestions to get you thinking.

- Share with a good friend why you decided to follow Jesus and what He means to you.
- Ask the Lord if there is a specific place He would like to send you to be His witness. Consider who you could invite to go with you.
- Determine to go through an entire day with "open eyes" looking for someone whom you could encourage or bless (do something nice for or show goodness to) in some way.
- Read through the Book of Mark (this will take a bit of time) and consider how you would help a friend who doesn't know much about Jesus, understand who Jesus is and what He is all about.

Pray this prayer of surrender to the Lord.

Father, I abandon myself into Your hands,
Do with me what You will,
Whatever you do, I will thank You,
I am ready for all, I accept all,
Let only Your will be done in me,
As in all Your Creatures, and I'll ask nothing else, my Lord.

Into Your hands I commend my spirit; I give it to You
With all the love of my heart,
For I love You, Lord,
And so need to give myself,
To surrender myself into Your hands
With a trust beyond all measure,
Because You are my Father

—Charles de Foucauld

It is not so much about trying to fit God into your life as figuring out how your life fits into God's.

Reflect

What action to help you "Go" did you choose?

What was the best thing about the experience?

What went poorly?

How does what you did connect or fit in with God's work of bringing about restoration to all the earth?

> *"I consider that our present sufferings are not worth comparing with the glory that will be revealed in us. The creation waits in eager expectation for the sons of God to be revealed. For the creation was subjected to frustration, not by its own choice, but by the will of the one who subjected it, in hope that the creation itself will be liberated from its bondage to decay and brought into the glorious freedom of the children of God."*
>
> —Romans 8:18-21

Talk

Gather together and share some food. Don't take your friends for granted. Allow yourself to feel a sense of gratitude for this family of friends you are a part of. These are your people.

Gather in groups of 3-4 and share with one another how your week has been. Consider giving each person a chance to share their "high and low" from the past week.

Give everyone a chance to share their reflections from the *Reflect* section.

Close in prayer. As you pray for one another remember to give God thanks for the good things that were shared. Also take time to pray for the struggles and things that didn't go so well.

End your prayer time by praying the Lord's Prayer together.

THE WAY OF
STORY

DAY 4

Transform

"Therefore, I urge you, brothers, in view of God's mercy, to offer your bodies as living sacrifices, holy and pleasing to God—this is your spiritual act of worship. Do not conform any longer to the pattern of this world, but be transformed by the renewing of your mind. Then you will be able to test and approve what God's will is—his good, pleasing and perfect will."

—Romans 12:1-2

One of the things that prevents growth and transformation in our lives is our own stubbornness, especially when it comes to sin.

I remember one of the first times I was trying to help my dad water the flowers in our garden. I went to get the water hose and stretched it out down the side of our house and into the back yard where the flowers were. By the time I got to the flower bed there was barely a trickle of water coming out of the hose. I could not figure out why. My dad was standing nearby and told me to follow him. He immediately started following the hose back toward the spigot where the water came out. About halfway there we came to a spot where the hose got tangled up in a knot. The hose was pinched nearly closed and prevented the water from flowing freely. As soon as I straightened out the hose, taking the kink out of it, the water began to flow freely once again.

Our lives are like that water hose. God's Spirit or Presence is like the water. Sin in our lives is like the knot or kink in the hose, preventing God's Spirit from flowing freely through us. Only when we get our lives "straightened out" can God's Spirit flow through us without interruption.

Is there any area of your life that you need to confess to God and bring under His submission? For most of us, it is not a long list of things, but only one or two things we stubbornly hold onto that are keeping us from experiencing more

of God's pleasure and power in our lives. What is the one thing you have been stubborn about holding on to, rather than surrendering it to God?

If it is something you have been struggling with for a while and you are really tired of it controlling you, then consider who in your community you could confess your sin to. James 5:16 teaches us, *"Therefore confess your sins to each other and pray for each other so that you may be healed."*

I have found that when I keep my sin to myself, it remains hidden and I remain powerless to overcome it. However, when I confess it to others and bring it out into the light, the sin begins to lose its power over me and I begin to experience "healing" and freedom from that sin.

Rest

"Trust in the Lord *and do good;*
dwell in the land and enjoy safe pasture.

Delight yourself in the Lord
and he will give you the desires of your heart.

Commit your way to the Lord*;*
trust in him and he will do this:

He will make your righteousness shine like the dawn,
the justice of your cause like the noonday sun.

Be still before the Lord *and wait patiently for him."*

—Psalm 37:4-7

Make a list of 10 things you are thankful for.

1.

2.

3.

4.

5.

6.

7.

8.

9.

10.

DAY 1

Preview

We've already tried to make it clear that a sacred community exists to embody and testify to the redemptive power of God at work in the world. We embody the redemptive power of God when our lives are Good News to others. When our community is known by love rather than hate, people take notice. When we offer hope rather than stressing people out, when we shine light rather than bring darkness, people notice.

A sacred community (the Church) is created by God as a community of the Spirit. The Church is sent by the Father and the Son and the Spirit into the world to embody and testify to the Good News of Jesus Christ. Our primary means of embodying the Good News is love. Our primary way of testifying to the Good News of Jesus Christ is sharing our own stories and experiences with Jesus Christ. In other words, it is simply telling others what Jesus has done for you and what He means to you.

Take for example the woman Jesus met at the well in John 4. She had a personal encounter with Jesus. He changed her life from the inside out and the next thing we know she has taken off (in such a hurry she leaves her jar for collecting water behind) to go tell anyone who will listen about this amazing person who has changed her life. In other words, she simply told her story about knowing Jesus.

> *"Many of the Samaritans from that town believed in him because of the woman's testimony, 'He told me everything I ever did.'"*
>
> —John 4:39

Reminds me of Peter and John's story in Acts 4, when they are told to shut up about Jesus. Remember there response, *"For we cannot help speaking about what we have see and heard."* For Peter and John, Jesus was not an answer to a Sunday school lesson. He was not just someone they read about or were told to believe in. Jesus was a real person they knew, who changed their lives. They could not stop talking about this brilliant man who had rescued them and saved their lives. They had to tell their story.

How about the man born blind in John 9:1-12? After he was healed a huge argument broke out about Jesus. This man did not have a lot of information about Jesus, but he knew what Jesus had done for him. Listen to his story, "*He replied, 'Whether he is a sinner of not, I don't know. One thing I do know. I was blind but now I see!*" This man did not get caught up in arguing about Jesus, but he simply and quite powerfully tells what Jesus has done for him. He tells his story.

> Testify: to make a statement based on personal knowledge or belief: bear witness: to serve as evidence or proof

There is a huge difference between trying to convince another person to do or believe something and simply telling your story (testifying or bearing witness to what God has done and is doing in your life). Don't argue with people, but don't be shy about telling your story either.

Conversation 1:

Christian: Jesus is the only way to heaven and without Him, you will go to hell.

Friend: How do you know that?

Christian: It says so in the Bible.

Friend: Well, I don't believe in the Bible, it has lots of contradictions and made up stories.

Christian: No it doesn't. It is all true. It is the Bible.

Friend: I just don't think I can believe in a God who allows such evil and suffering to exist in our world.

Christian: God doesn't want those things to happen anymore than you or I do. There is suffering and evil in the world because of sin.

Friend: If God is so powerful, then why doesn't He do something to stop it?

Conversation 2:

Friend: What did you do this weekend?

You: I went with a group of friends from church to feed some hungry people at a homeless shelter.

Friend: Oh that sounds cool.

You: Yeah, it was a lot of fun.

Friend: It seems like you are always doing stuff like that, trying to help other people and stuff. How come?

You: I think because I know what it is like to need help or to feel lost.

Friend: What do you mean?

You: I used to feel sort of lost, like I didn't fit in anywhere. It was like my life was broken. Then Amanda started talking to me about Jesus and how Jesus had changed her life and made it so much better. Together we started reading the Gospel of Mark and I discovered that Jesus was really cool. I started going with her when they would go places like the homeless shelter and to church on Sunday mornings. After a while I really began to believe that God loved me. So I made the decision to follow Jesus and accept God's love and forgiveness.

Friend: Oh, I see (she doesn't really, but that's ok, she's trying to be polite). So what's it been like?

You: It has been great. It's like nothing has changed and everything has changed all at the same time. Since I began following Jesus I have this strong feeling that God loves me and is with me. I don't feel lost or broken anymore. I'm also learning to think more about other people and not just myself.

Friend: Oh that sounds cool. I gotta get going.

You: Yeah me too. Hey next time we go to the homeless shelter, would you want to come with?

Friend: Yeah, maybe. I'll have to think about it.

What is the difference between the two conversations?

Are either of them realistic? Why or why not?

Both Jesus and the early church community embodied and proclaimed the Good News. What does that mean? They testified to the greatness of God by their words as well as their actions. The New Testament scholar NT Wright points out that Jesus' primary method of delivering his message was by His actions. (He was the "word made flesh.") However, He then used stories (parables) and metaphor to explain the meaning of His actions.

Like any healthy body, the church needs to use both verbal and non-verbal means of communicating. It is right and good for us to boldly proclaim the good news of Jesus Christ. We ought to be telling the story of His life, death, and resurrection. We better be sharing our stories of how we too are dying to self and being raised up to new life. However if our lives do not match our message, what do you think people are going to believe? Non-verbal communication has always carried more weight than verbal communication. People need to see that your life is good news, before they will listen to you talk about the Good News.

Your words should not be used to try to convince people that Jesus is the way, but rather to help others understand why you are living the way of Jesus. (The job of convincing is the Holy Spirit's, John 16:8.) Tell stories of why you trust God. Share boldly why you love Him so. Shout praise to God at the next sight of a beautiful sunset. Give thanks the next time you have food to eat.

You are His witness. You have been called to testify. What is your story?

Meditate

Get out your Bible and carefully read through Paul's story as told in Acts 26:1-23.

Before you begin reading take a moment to draw closer to God.

> **The more we call on God**
> **the more we can feel God's presence.**
> **Day by day we are drawn closer**
> **to the loving heart of God.**
> **(Taken from www.sacredgateway.com)**

Then Agrippa said to Paul, "You have permission to speak for yourself."

So Paul motioned with his hand and began his defense: "King Agrippa, I consider myself fortunate to stand before you today as I make my defense against all the accusations of the Jews, and especially so because you are well acquainted with all the Jewish customs and controversies. Therefore, I beg you to listen to me patiently.

"The Jewish people all know ***the way I have lived*** *ever since I was a child, from the beginning of* ***my life*** *in my own country, and also in Jerusalem. They have known me for a long time and can* ***testify****, if they are willing, that I conformed to the strictest sect of our religion, living as a Pharisee. And now it is because of my hope in what God has promised our ancestors that I am on trial today. This is the promise our twelve tribes are hoping to see fulfilled as they earnestly serve God day and night. King Agrippa, it is because of this hope that the Jews are accusing me. Why should any of you consider it incredible that God raises the dead?*

"I too was convinced that I ought to do all that was possible to oppose the name of Jesus of Nazareth. And that is just what I did in Jerusalem. On the authority of the chief priests I put

many of the Lord's people in prison, and when they were put to death, I cast my vote against them. Many a time I went from one synagogue to another to have them punished, and I tried to force them to blaspheme. I was so obsessed with persecuting them that I even hunted them down in foreign cities.

"On one of these journeys I was going to Damascus with the authority and commission of the chief priests. About noon, King Agrippa, as I was on the road, I saw a light from heaven, brighter than the sun, blazing around me and my companions. We all fell to the ground, and I heard a voice saying to me in Aramaic, 'Saul, Saul, why do you persecute me? It is hard for you to kick against the goads.'

"Then I asked, 'Who are you, Lord?'

"'I am Jesus, whom you are persecuting,' the Lord replied. 'Now get up and stand on your feet. I have appeared to you to appoint you as a servant and as a witness of what you have seen and will see of me. I will rescue you from your own people and from the Gentiles. I am sending you to them to open their eyes and turn them from darkness to light, and from the power of Satan to God, so that they may receive forgiveness of sins and a place among those who are sanctified by faith in me.'

"So then, King Agrippa, I was not disobedient to the vision from heaven. First to those in Damascus, then to those in Jerusalem and in all Judea, and then to the Gentiles, I preached that they should repent and turn to God and demonstrate their repentance by their deeds. That is why some Jews seized me in the temple courts and tried to kill me. But God has helped me to this very day; so I stand here and testify to small and great alike. I am saying nothing beyond what the prophets and Moses said would happen—that the Messiah would suffer and, as the first to rise from the dead, would bring the message of light to his own people and to the Gentiles."

—Acts 26:1-23, emphasis added

Go back to the story and place a B.C. next to the section where Paul is talking about his life before Jesus. Place a + (cross) next to the section where he talks about his encounter with Jesus.

Place an A.D. next in the margins next to where he explains what his life is like now that He has surrendered to Jesus.

This chapter is about the way of Story. The story of God and how our smaller stories fit within God's Grand Story. One of the things we want this chapter to do is to help you know how to share your story with others. It isn't hard, but sometimes we don't know how to organize our thoughts. Perhaps this will help. One way to organize your story is to think of it in three parts.

- **Part 1: B.C.** (before Christ). What your life was like before you were following Jesus.
- **Part 2: Surrender to Jesus.** The point where you surrender to Jesus.
- **Part 3: A.D.** "Anno Domini" which means "in the year of our Lord." What your life is like now that you are following Jesus.

(Note this pattern occurs over and over again in each area of your life as you continue to grow and surrender more and more of your life to Him.)

Let's see how these three categories look when applied to Paul's story as told in Acts 26.

Part 1: B.C.

How would you describe Paul's life before he meets Christ? (vv. 4-11)

Part 2: Surrender to Jesus

Make a list of things you notice about Paul's encounter of surrendering to Jesus. (vv. 12-18)

Part 3: A.D.

Describe Paul's life now that he is following Jesus. How is he different? What has changed?

Act

What's Your Story?

Yesterday we looked at a simple way of organizing your story by breaking it up into three parts.

1. Life before Christ (BC)
2. Surrender to Jesus (+)
3. Life with Christ (AD)

Today we want to turn our attention from Paul's story to your story. Using the same three categories, write out your story below. You can either do a broad overview of your life, giving a general account or pick a specific area of your life God has been working on lately. (For example, the way you treat your parents, the way you talk about others, how you spend your time and so on.)

Part 1: B.C.

What was your life like before you began following Jesus?

Part 2: Surrender to Jesus

Describe your experience of meeting Jesus and making the decision to trust Him as your Lord and Savior

Part 3: A.D.

What is your life like now that Jesus is your Lord? How has following Jesus made a difference in your life?

Who can you tell?

Now think of at least two people with whom you could share your story. The first person should be someone with whom you feel very safe as well as someone you can tell your story to today either in person or over the phone. Maybe it is one of your parents, your best friend or your youth worker from church. Write down the name of the person with whom you are going to share your story.

The second person could be someone with whom you have never shared your story. Maybe it is someone from school who knows you go to church and are a Christian, but you've never told them about your story of coming to follow Jesus. Perhaps now God will use you to explain why you are different from so many of the other students at school. Perhaps God wants you to "testify" to His goodness, His power, and His love for all His children.

Pray and ask God to lead you to someone with whom you can share. Trust Him to give you the words and courage. During the next several days, look for opportunities to share your story. God will provide the opportunity, but it is up to you to not miss it.

Now go tell the person whose name you wrote down.

Reflect

What do you make of the fact that one of the results of Paul courageously and relentlessly sharing his story was that it landed him in jail? What does that say about his passion for Jesus and His Way?

Another of the results of Paul's life and story is that the Good News of Jesus spread like fire all over the world. How do you think that realization made Paul feel?

If Paul were standing before you right now, do you think he would say that being beaten, abandoned, forgotten, and thrown in jail was worth so many people being rescued by Jesus through his testimony and life?

How do you feel about your story? How do you feel about being called to testify about the reality of God in our world today?

How much are you willing to suffer for telling your story?

Can you imagine God using you, like He did Paul, to accomplish His purposes in the world? How would that make you feel?

> *"For we know, brothers loved by God, that he has chosen you, because our gospel came to you not simply with words, but also with power, with the Holy Spirit and with deep conviction. You know how we lived among you for your sake. You became imitators of us and of the Lord; in spite of severe suffering, you welcomed the message with the joy given by the Holy Spirit. And so you became a model to all the believers in Macedonia and Achaia. The Lord's message rang out from you not only in Macedonia and Achaia—your faith in God has become known everywhere. Therefore we do not need to say anything about it, for they themselves report what kind of reception you gave us. They tell how you turned to God from idols to serve the living and true God, and to wait for his Son from heaven, whom he raised from the dead—Jesus, who rescues us from the coming wrath."*
>
> —1 Thessalonians 1:2-10

Talk

Play a game and share a meal together.

After everyone has had a chance to grab some food, get something to drink, and gather in groups of 3-4. Go around the circle, giving everyone a chance to share their "high" and "low" from the past few days. When everyone has had a chance to share have one or two people pray for the group, keeping in mind what has just been shared.

Next give everyone a chance to share their story, using the B.C., +, and A.D. categories. After a person finishes telling their story, they should share with the group how they would complete the following three sentences.

One thing I am learning about myself lately is ________________

____

One thing I could use some help with is ________________

____

One thing I am thankful for is ________________________

____

When everyone has had their turn, use the Lord's Prayer to close your time together.

Transform

"I waited patiently for the Lord*;*
he turned to me and heard my cry.

He lifted me out of the slimy pit,
out of the mud and mire;
he set my feet on a rock
and gave me a firm place to stand.

He put a new song in my mouth,
a hymn of praise to our God.
Many will see and fear
and put their trust in the Lord*.*

Blessed is the man
who makes the Lord *his trust,*
who does not look to the proud,
to those who turn aside to false gods."

—Psalm 40:1-4

Read through the above passage again and circle any words that stand out to you.

When you ponder the words you have circled, how do they make you feel?

Are there any ways this testimony from the psalmist is like your own story? In what ways are they similar? In what ways are they different?

Take a few minutes to consider how your life might be different if it were not for God's grace and rescuing presence in your life.

Consider writing your own psalm of transformation. Feel free to use Psalm 42 as a pattern.

> *"As for you, you were dead in your transgressions and sins, in which you used to live when you followed the ways of this world and of the ruler of the kingdom of the air, the spirit who is now at work in those who are disobedient. All of us also lived among them at one time, gratifying the cravings of our sinful nature and following its desires and thoughts. Like the rest, we were by nature objects of wrath. But because of his great love for us, God, who is rich in mercy, made us alive with Christ even when we were dead in transgressions—it is by grace you have been saved. And God raised us up with Christ and seated us with him in the heavenly realms in Christ Jesus, in order that in the coming ages he might show the incomparable riches of his grace, expressed in his kindness to us in Christ Jesus. For it is by grace you have been saved, through faith—and this not from yourselves, it is the gift of God—not by works, so that no one can boast. For we are God's workmanship, created in Christ Jesus to do good works, which God prepared in advance for us to do."* —Ephesians 2:1-10

Rest

"It will be a sign between me and the Israelites forever, for in six days the Lord *made the heavens and the earth, and on the seventh day he abstained from work and rested."* —Exodus 31:17

"Be strong and let your heart take courage, all you who ***wait*** *for the* Lord*."*
—Psalm 31:24, emphasis added

The idea behind the word "wait" is that the one waiting is confident that God will show up to help and rescue. The marks of those who wait for the Lord in this manner are strength, courage and hope.

"I wait for the Lord*, my soul*
waits,
and in his word I put my
hope."
—Psalm 130:5

"The King and all the people who were with him arrived weary at the Jordan; and there he refreshed himself." —2 Samuel 16:14

"I'll wait as long as he says.
Everything I need comes from him, so
why not?
He's solid rock under my feet,
breathing room *for my soul,*
an impregnable castle:
I'm set for life."
—Psalm 62:1, MSG, emphasis added

"Come to me, all you who are weary and burdened, and I will give you rest."

—Jesus, Matthew 11:28

www.ingramcontent.com/pod-product-compliance
Lightning Source LLC
Chambersburg PA
CBHW060018050426
42448CB00012B/2808

* 9 7 8 0 8 3 4 1 5 0 3 8 6 *